BACKYARD
AND
BEYOND

There were trees blowing, standing still, growing, knowing, whose names I never knew. (Once, indeed, with a friend I wrote a poem beginning, "All trees are oaks, except fir trees.") There were birds being busy, or sleep-flying, in the sky. (The poem had continued, "All birds are robins, except crows or rooks.") Nature was doing what it was doing, and thinking just that.

—Dylan Thomas,
The Crumbs of One Man's Year

BACKYARD
AND
BEYOND

A Guide for
Discovering the Outdoors

Edward Duensing
A. B. Millmoss

FULCRUM PUBLISHING
GOLDEN, COLORADO

Copyright © 1992
Edward Duensing and Millmoss Associates

Cover design by Ann E. Green, Green Design

All Rights Reserved

Library of Congress Cataloging-in-Publication Data

Duensing, Edward.
    Backyard and beyond : a guide for discovering the
outdoors / Edward Duensing, A.B. Millmoss.
        p.   cm.
    Includes bibliographical references (p.) and
index.
    ISBN 1-55591-071-8 (pbk.)
    1. Nature study. 2. Tracking and trailing.
I. Millmoss, A.B. II. Title.
QH51.D84   1992
508—dc20   91-58485
                                              CIP

Printed in the United States of America

0   9   8   7   6   5   4   3   2   1

Fulcrum Publishing
350 Indiana Street, Suite 350
Golden, Colorado 80401

To Lennie and Sy,

pathfinders in their own fields

CONTENTS

INTRODUCTION

*To a person uninstructed in natural history,
his country or seaside stroll is a walk through a
gallery filled with wonderful works, nine-tenths
of which have their faces turned to the wall.*
—T. H. Huxley

S o much of nature is marked "hide in plain sight." The people we venerate have learned to look deeply. They have traveled much in Concord, like Thoreau, or have visited distant lands like Darwin, and have altered our perception of nature. When we try the same, we go clumping off into the woods after Nature with a capital *N*, only to find the woods oddly silent except for our own breathing. We have arrived to find the pictures turned to the wall. We need a little instruction.

To this end, we have written a travel book for the woods and fields. The writer is A. B. Millmoss, and the naturalist is Edward Duensing. What we present here is a how-to guide for the weekend naturalist. It shows you how

to see wildlife on your own half-acre plot or in a national
park, in a swamp or on a mountain top. The emphasis is
on practical information about common plants, animals
and habitats. There are no long equipment lists and few
Latin names. It is not a field manual for strict identification
after the fact; it is, rather, a kind of "owner's manual" for
your backyard or local woods. It's a book for those who
might agree with Dylan Thomas when he once wrote that
all trees were firs except oaks and all birds robins, except
crows or rooks.

There is, as we all suspect, a whole lot more going on
about us than we realize. But getting closer to it is another
story. It is fine to read that there may be otters or Monarch
butterflies around, but the question is: Where does one
begin to look for them? There are a pair of tracks across the
snow, but whose are they? Here we reintroduce the
common sense of the woods: why you may be less likely to
be spotted if you hide in front of a large rock or tree rather
than behind it; where deer never look and where you
should hide; how to walk quietly in the woods; the best
places and times of day to see wildlife. And we examine
some of the smaller signposts: what a dry turtle in your
path may mean, and which animal leaves mushrooms in
trees as a calling card. After walking about, carefully
looking, we can begin to see the near-at-hand closely. See
that there is no actual nightfall. See the changes in bird
flight that presage bad weather.

All these things are there to be seen, but they're not
visible until you learn to look for them, learn to turn the
paintings around.

The whole trick is learning to hide in plain sight.
Thoreau, as always, said it best. He wrote in *Walden*, "It is
remarkable how many creatures live wild and free though
secret in the woods, and still sustain themselves in the
neighborhood of towns, suspected by hunters only. How
retired the otter manages to live here! He grows to be four

feet long, as big as a small boy, perhaps without any human being getting a glimpse of him." And then he tells of watching in one clearing a raccoon, a red squirrel, woodcocks and turtle doves, and concludes: "You only need to sit still long enough in some attractive spot in the woods that all its inhabitants may exhibit themselves to you by turns."

Just "sit still long enough" says Thoreau. But how long? He spent his life observing and still didn't see it all. He walked through the fields around Concord, identifying, labeling and describing the hidden mysteries of the ordinary. Natural history is about naming the land. This tree, that track. The earth at this spot formed this way and this is what lives here now. Here is the story, the narrative. Here is our place in it. To learn a little of our surroundings is to join in the story.

1

STALKING

Hide in Plain Sight

In the woods and fields we are tourists in a foreign
country. If we are the stereotypical tourists, we will be
blinded by our swagger, and end up looking at other
tourists who are looking at the well-known "tourist site."
It is distressing to journey so far to see only others like
yourself. If we have learned to travel, we will find the places
where the laundry is hung out, where life is really lived.
And that's what travel is all about—to see how others are
living.

In our national parks we usually behave like the
guidebook-blinded tourist. You can hear the way we view
a "site." We hop out of our cars, camera in hand, walk up,
click-click-click, a hillside of mechanical crickets, or if it's
home movies, *whirr-whirrr*, then perhaps a pose in front of
the geyser, rock outcrop or scenic overlook, a glance at the
historic marker and then with a final swivel of the head we
offer the tourists' benediction: "It's beautiful, it's gorgeous,
where to next?" This is how most of us view the parks.

The park rangers have a term for us—"windshield
visitors," because we rarely leave our cars. From behind

1

our windshields we have not seen where nature hangs its laundry out. We have stopped at the marked sites, the handrail-and-macadam-path sites, as if they were stations of the cross. We have seen little more than a succession of 3-D postcards.

The goal then is to become travelers, to return not with a handful of slides of the known, expected sites, but to return ready to share many observations about the locals. In the woods, of course, the locals are the animals and plants.

This chapter is not about what you must see, it is about *how* to see. It is a lesson on traveling in the exotic country of your own backyard. The rewards are great when we bring the adventuring spirit reserved for foreign travel into our daily lives and our nearby woods and fields.

There are a few techniques to be learned that will have a high return once you are off in the woods. These are refinements of, or reintroductions to, our common sense. There are two ways of going after wildlife: in posting, you let the animal come to you, whereas in stalking, you follow the animal. To post an area successfully, you must choose your hiding spot well, conceal yourself and your scent, and most important, hone your patience to the point where you can sit stone-still. To stalk an animal, a careful woods-walk has to be learned, as does an alertness to the "news" in the woods. This requires re-educating the senses of hearing, sight and smell. But first, as with any trip, it is important to know where and when to go.

The Best Places and Times to Go

Seek times and areas of change. Nature reveals itself most where woods meet meadow, in spring and fall, and at dawn and dusk.

Ecotones, the places where two different environments meet, will be home to plants and animals from both distinct environments, as well as species that dwell only in these marginal habitats. The areas around ponds and at the edges of woods and the estuaries of rivers are particularly good natural intersections. For example, at a pond's edge you'll find fish in the shallow water, raccoons on the bank and frogs hopping in between the shallows and the shore.

Lands managed for game, in the off-hunting seasons, are good places to seek out wildlife. Often this land is managed to maximize the amount of "edge," or ecotones. Fields are cut to leave alternating strips of grass and brush. And out of hunting season no one thinks to venture there.

Every animal has a preferred habitat. Know the habitat and you'll know which animals and plants you'll find there. You won't find many robins or meadowlarks in the deep woods, nor will you find many nuthatches or kingfishers in a dry, treeless field. Often, I've located the ponds in the woods by listening for the red-winged blackbirds that nest near water. Plants can be good clues to altitude. Pearly everlastings, small white plants that grow rampant all over the province of Quebec, are found only on the mountains of our Middle Atlantic states. Also, many plants common in the high elevations of the South are found only in valleys in the North.

In the spring and fall animals are on the move and, therefore, more visible. In these seasons you can get a glimpse of many birds that are just passing through. And with the leaves gone in early spring and late fall, more animals will be exposed to view. The woods in early spring also offer some of the most colorful flowers, such as wake-robin (*Trillium erectum*) and trout lily (*Erythronium americanum*), which blossom brilliantly during their brief chance for sun, before they are shaded out by the trees overhead.

At dawn and dusk both diurnal and nocturnal spe-

cies are active. During these changes of shifts, the awaking
animals will be out foraging after their rest, and the other
animals will be heading home.

As you become aware of the plants and animals
around, you will be more attuned to the passing of time.
Before long you will begin to identify certain sounds out of
the familiar but nonspecific background noises you have
always heard: wild turkeys yelping in the morning, cicidas
buzzing on hot summer afternoons, peepers singing in the
spring evenings, Canada geese honking their way south in
the fall. There are quieter signs as well: chickory blossoms
and coneflowers close by noon, while dandelions wait until
dusk to fold up their petals. Dames rockets and evening
primrose are fragrant only after dusk, when many of
daytime's most fragrant blossoms have lost their scent.

Posting

"All good things come to those who wait" is an old
saying, and one which is proved true in the woods. One of
the best ways to observe animals is to sit still at an
inconspicuous spot with a good view of the surrounding
area. By sitting quietly you can observe an amazing
number of shy and flighty animals that would have fled or
taken cover if you had been walking through.

First you must place yourself for the wait.

Vantage Points

Take the high ground. Always try to have a clear view
of the surrounding area.

Few animals look for danger above them as often as
they look to their flanks and rear. Ideally, locate yourself
at heights of around 10 feet or more. Deer will graze
unawares right below, if you just sit still.

When going to your vantage point, it is usually better to move along a trail, rather than thrash through the brush. On a trail you can move more quickly and quietly, and you won't be intruding on the territories of the animals you hope to observe.

Trees are good lookout posts. To make a quiet ascent, grab and climb onto branches where they join the tree trunk; they are much less apt to break or creak at these junctions. Don't put all your weight on a branch at once; test it first.

Your parked car can also serve as an excellent blind. Many animals will not be the least bit shy of approaching a stationary automobile. However, the woods are not the drive-in movies and there are some things you simply will not be able to see from a car.

Cover, Concealment and Camouflage

Begin your concealment when you dress. Wear loose, bulky clothing that will break up your outline. These are less likely to bind than tight-fitting clothes, and will be more comfortable to sit still in.

Your clothing should match the shade and color of the area you'll be in. Wear patterned or camouflaged clothing to break up your outline. By wearing a red-and-black-checkered jacket, or pants and jacket of different colors, your form will be broken down into different pieces, harder for animals to detect. Although most animals are color-blind, they are sensitive to differences in shade.

In cold weather wear layers of clothing instead of one heavy coat. Sweaters and heavy flannel shirts will keep in body heat, and wind-proof outerwear will keep out the chill of the air. With layered clothing you are dressed for a wide range of temperatures. You can remove a couple of layers for a hike in the sun, then put them back on for a long sit in the shade.

There are many ways to hide in the woods. One way is right out in the open: hide in plain sight. Place yourself in front of an object (a large tree or rock) rather than behind it. When you hide behind something, you give yourself away every time you peer around or over it, telegraphing your movements to the animals in the area.

Two things to be avoided when posting are movement and anything that, even for an instant, defines your outline. If your clothes blend in well and you can sit still, you will be concealed—right out in the open. Always make sure that your equipment isn't reflecting light and giving away your position.

If you sit *alongside* a tree or other large object when trying to conceal yourself, your every move will be visible to an animal. Sit with your back up against the tree. This will not leave you silhouetted against the sky, and it will mask your small movements. It is also the most comfortable position, providing a backrest, and the more comfortable you are, the longer you can sit still. Similarly, when hiding by the crest of a ridge, sit beneath the crest, not on top of it, where you will be silhouetted by the sky or moon.

When hiding behind a tree, or other cover, never peek around the side while standing. This will put your face in full view for the animal to see. Instead, lie down on the ground and look through the undergrowth that surrounds your cover. Move only when your quarry is distracted, and move slowly. Never move an entire branch to look through a bush or tree. You may as well wave a flag and say, "Hey, look over here." Instead, part a few leaves with your fingertips.

Try to remain in shadowed areas. On a bright day the contrast between shade and a sunny area will help to hide you. Avoid strong light, which from any angle will make you more visible. Light falling on your back creates a rim of light along your silhouette, making you as visible as a blinking neon sign in the woods.

Your own shadow may also give you away. It can stretch out in front of you as you move, scaring every animal in the area.

Nothing will betray you more than your face and hands. A flourish of the hands will reveal your position. Animals are quick to pick up on such movements. Just as nature chose a white tail to alert other deer, moving hands stand out against the ground. Darken your face, if possible, and always keep your hands still and covered in your lap or under your jacket. By sticking fern leaves or grass into your hat or headband you can break up your outline— but this can also be a drawback, as the leaves will accent every move you make with your head.

Any quick movement or careless sound will undo your long patient sit. Always move slowly and smoothly, avoiding any jerky stop-and-start movement.

Sitting still takes practice. You cannot remain immobile by trying to keep your muscles stiffly in place. To keep still, your body should be relaxed, not tense.

Try the following technique to perfect quietude. First, concentrate on relaxing the muscles in your arms, your legs and the rest of your body. Next, concentrate on keeping your tongue from touching your teeth, while keeping your tongue relaxed, almost floating, or concentrate on touching your tongue to the roof of your mouth. Then, let your eyelid muscles relax, and concentrate on this relaxed feeling while scanning the terrain. It is surprising at first how effective this concentration on your eyelids and tongue is in keeping the rest of your body relaxed and motionless.

To remain motionless for a longer period of time, learn to concentrate on your breathing. Inhale slowly through your nose, filling the lower lungs first and swelling the abdomen. Then slowly fill them up the rest of the way, expanding your chest cavity. When your lungs are full, exhale, letting the air slip slowly out through your mouth.

Empty the chest cavity first, and finally push out the last of it by contracting your abdomen. Be careful not to make any noise. Breathing this way will relax your mind and body, enabling you to stay still even longer.

When sitting still, an impending sneeze or cough becomes a big event, threatening to give you away. To control a sneeze, firmly press your forefinger against the point where your upper lip and nose meet. While this is effective, it is something of a trade-off, because it requires that you move your hand up in front of your face, an action sure to expose you to the wary eyes of wild animals. A better—if more unlikely—method is to try pinching the top of your thigh midway between your knee and your hip; this will stop the sneeze and let you keep your hands low and covered.

To suppress a cough, lightly pinch your Adam's apple. This takes practice. Too much pressure will increase your need to cough, but just enough pressure will stop it.

The length of time to spend posting an area depends on what you feel up to that day, your luck in seeing wildlife and your patience. A good rule of thumb is to stay through your first bout of boredom. After that, you're likely to settle down. Sitting still for less than ten or fifteen minutes is not likely to be productive. Most animals are not going to forget you are there. Generally, I'll stay until I've seen something. One day a fawn walked up close enough for me to touch her. Once in a snowstorm chickadees alighted on my shoulders. And another time a mink came up to within an inch of my foot and we sat regarding each other. Posting is like fishing, and practice will tell you how long to leave the bait in the water. Some days, though, are made for rambling, not sitting still.

Patience

Modern life affords many opportunities for you to develop patience. While waiting in line at the bank or supermarket, or waiting in your car at a red light or in a traffic jam, you can develop the patience that will increase the length of time you can sit still in the woods. Patience is a skill. You can cultivate stillness in mind and body. While waiting, practice the relaxation and breathing techniques previously mentioned. Another good exercise is to count your breaths: 1-2-3-4, and back again.

Scent

On a calm day the scent from a stationary human will build up and spread out in a circle of up to 25 feet, depending on terrain and weather conditions. If the wind is right an animal will be able to smell you long before it can see you. However, the spread of the scent is omnidirectional and the animal won't be able to pinpoint your position if you remain still.

The best way to mask your scent is to remain downwind of your quarry. Try to approach your vantage point so the wind is blowing toward you, carrying your scent to the rear, away from the area you're watching. (Sound also carries downwind.)

To determine the direction of a light breeze, wet your finger in your mouth and hold it aloft over your head. Soon one side of your finger will feel noticeably cooler—this will be the direction the breeze is blowing from. You can also drop some dust from your pockets and watch as the breeze deflects its fall.

More dedicated naturalists often take greater pains to mask their scent. They will rub strong-smelling plants such as balsam needles, honeysuckle flowers or pennyroyal leaves on their body and clothes. Or they'll crush an apple and rub it on their boot soles, and then crush another to use as a lure, throwing it to the place they'll be watching for animals.

Some hardcore naturalists take a more direct approach to get the smell of the outdoors into their clothes. They thoroughly wash their clothes, leave them out to dry, and then store them in a box full of leaves, hay or aromatic wood chips.

Calling Animals

Some days it takes a little prodding as well as waiting to get good things to come your way. Now and then you need to make some noise to get the world's attention. There are several tricks that can sometimes entice animals to come forward and show themselves.

By making a squeaking sound like that of a bird or mouse in trouble I have attracted hawks, foxes, raccoons, feral housecats and all manner of birds. Wet a spot on the back of your hand with saliva. Then suck on that spot to make a squeaking sound. This call should be urgent and intense, but don't overdo it or the animals will become suspicious. Call for a few seconds, pause for a few minutes, then try calling again. Some birds will still ignore you, no matter how good you are at this. So if a bird you want to see remains hidden in the bush, try a low-pitched hiss. This will sometimes flush the bird out.

Another way to make a loud squeaking sound is to hold a broad blade of grass taut between your up-pointing thumbs and blow on it. If you are holding the grass correctly, the squeak will stop squirrels and chipmunks in their tracks and attract curious birds and predators.

With two small, smooth stones you can imitate the chatter of a squirrel gnawing on a nut. Rubbing or tapping the stones lightly together will often attract chipmunks and squirrels—and occasionally a rabbit.

Sometimes appealing in a more general way to an animal's curiosity will succeed. Softly scratching the ground or the bark of a tree may draw a creature out for a look.

When you call to animals, don't expect them to come to you across open ground. They will usually move toward you along the route that provides them the best cover. The more cautious take a circuitous route as they try to move in a favorable direction to pick up a scent in the wind. A white-tailed buck will usually walk just inside the treeline near a clearing, rather than through the clearing itself.

Now and then an animal might even call to you. Once I was startled by a sneezing-coughing sound, quite like a person who had inhaled pepper. I turned to see a sizable buck. Indignant at being spotted, but still coughing, he moved off quickly.

After you've sat a while, you'll want to hit the trail to see what you can see. And you'll see much more if you know how to stalk your quarry.

Stalking

Stalking, the dictionary tells us, has a synonym in the word *steal*. We have to be that furtive, secretive, stealthy; we are stealing glimpses of life in the woods and meadows. We have to wait it out, as in posting, and sneak up on it to catch life unawares. We must remove ourselves from the scene as much as possible; we want to be the observer, not the observed. Successful stalking depends on seeing your quarry before it sees you.

The Stalker's Walk

To walk silently through the woods takes a few adjustments of our regular gait.

In our daily march through life, the body develops a forward momentum as weight is transferred to the leading heel ("thump") and the foot rolls to the ground ("flap"). The trailing leg is kept straight and brought forward, the back edge of the heel first ("thump") and then the rest of the foot ("flap"). Walking this way in a quiet meadow we tap out our presence.

The stalker's walk requires that you redistribute your weight. The trailing knee is kept slightly bent and the body's weight is kept over the rear leg until a good (noiseless) spot is found to set down the leading foot. As you bring the leading foot in for a landing, keep most of the weight on the rear leg. First gently set down the outer edge of the ball of the foot, next come down on the entire outside edge, then roll your foot slowly toward the arch.

Before you take your next step, check for any leaves or twigs that will amplify the sound of your movements. Shift your weight to the recently planted forward foot, and slowly bring the rear foot to the lead. This will keep your weight on the rear leg, allowing you to freeze instantly. You will also be able to change your mind at the last moment, since you can practically float the lead foot to the quietest spot.

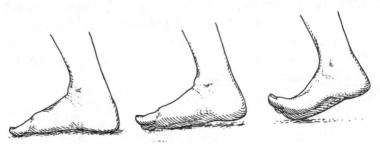

Stalker's walk

As you do this, remember to lift your feet well up off the ground to avoid rubbing against the low-lying plants that make a telltale shuffling-rustling sound. This should also keep you from tripping.

Don't be put off by this description. Any continuous fluid motion sounds more complicated than it really is when it is broken down into parts. Turning a door knob and opening a door is a simple, automatic movement; but imagine having to describe each separate twist, pull and push. Once practiced, the stalker's walk will be as natural as opening a door.

One problem, though, is that in moving this slowly, you can lose your balance. To remedy this, swing the forward-moving rear foot in an arc, toward the supporting leg, rather than straight ahead. This gives you much more stability.

The stalker's walk is ideal for closing in on animals, but you may want to move more quickly. A modified stalker's walk will take you swiftly and quietly on your way. Keep some of your weight on your bent, trailing leg. Bring your forward heel down with as little weight on it as possible and roll the front of your foot down, along the outside edge of your sole. All the while, you are transferring your weight from rear to front, as with the slower walk. It is important that you *roll* your foot down rather than slap-flapping it down. As you move, always try to keep your footsteps rhythmic. And pause frequently to look and listen for animals.

The techniques of posting also apply here: restrain the movement of your head and hands, so as not to alarm animals. Try to blend in with the background. Don't let your shadow give you away. Try to hide it in some cover. For example, let your shadow fall on some brush, or be sure your shadow is obscured by the larger shadow of some other object. The goal is not to let your quarry see the form or movement of your shadow. Keep close to the earth, especially when coming over a rise, and keep downwind.

Seeing

In stalking animals in the woods we are really on the lookout for a jigsaw puzzle of hints—shapes, stripes, movement. By using peripheral vision we can pick up such clues and assemble the pieces into a deer or a woodchuck.

Using peripheral vision will take a little practice. Direct your attention to the entire field of your vision. As you adjust to this way of seeing, you will notice movements off to the side and above that would have escaped your attention had you been staring straight ahead in a blindered fashion.

As an exercise, first train your eyes on an object in the middle distance, then examine the objects at the edge of your peripheral vision at varying distances. Concentrate on keeping this "wide scan" vision while walking, and soon it will come naturally.

When you notice something you want to study, direct your attention to it by bringing it into the sharpest area of vision. Then study the puzzle pieces—the shape of the parts, its texture, color and the tempo of its motion.

Don't expect to always see the whole animal. Be alert for exposed parts to tip you off—ears, legs, tails or patches of color that stand out while the rest is hidden. Look *into* the brush, not just around it, and look into the crosshatching of branches, not just above or below. Don't regard the woods as a solid object. Once you learn to notice what looks out of place, you'll see more animals.

In the woods and in thickets, keep an eye out for horizontal lines amid the vertical trees. You can do this systematically by looking above the trees and slowly bringing your eyes down, focusing on all you pass over, studying the horizontal lines. You'll see some large branches growing straight out and some fallen timber, but you may also find some hidden animals. This works particularly well with deer, elk, bears and other large mammals.

Scanning the lower vegetation will also give you a few hints. The emergent plant life that grows in the shallow waters around ponds, lakes and rivers will sometimes be alive with rustling leaves. Usually this will be from a large fish bumping into the plant's stems, but it can also be from a muskrat, turtle or water bird. Scanning can also work in a field of tall grass or any place an animal brushes against plants while moving. A fat woodchuck in a hayfield will give itself away every time.

To see larger animals you have to look farther afield.

The most important area to scan is the extreme range of terrain you can see. Many people concentrate only on the area immediately surrounding them. While this is a good way to see rabbits and song birds, it is also a sure way to miss the larger or more reclusive animals that will spot you and be long gone before you approach. Many animals don't wait until danger is on top of them before they flee. Some of these animals have superior eyesight, comparable to a human looking through 8x binoculars. So, in essence, think of yourself as if you were in a lookout duel, pitted against an opponent with binoculars. You will have to walk quietly and look far down the trail to spot your opponent first.

Whenever you come upon a ridge, clearing, lake or any place where the land opens to view, slow your pace and look first at the most distant ground. Then sweep your eyes across the ground closer to you. In this way I've caught sight of most of the foxes I've seen.

Hearing

The old movie matinée trick of keeping your ear to the ground works well to amplify the hoofbeats of large animals or the clomping of heavily booted people. But if you're not expecting a buffalo stampede or a cavalry charge to shake the earth, forget it. However, another old trick of those matinée idols does work. Cupping your hands behind your ears increases the size of the ear, and allows you to gather faint sounds. Again, compare yourself to the animals you are stalking; many of them have upright ears of considerable size that they can direct toward a sound. Cupping your ears will also help you determine the direction a sound is coming from. Keeping your mouth slightly open will allow you to hear low sounds somewhat clearer.

Try out your "stalker's ears" on two backyard ventriloquists, the cricket and the cicada. Listen first with the unaided ear. These creatures sound as if they are coming from everywhere except where they are. Cup your ears and the sound takes on a little more directional definition; now you can locate them. Next try locating birds in the brush.

Just as you opened your eyes to see to the farthest edge of your vision, so you have to open up your hearing. Make an effort to listen to all the sounds around you when you're afield. The background noise is not the Muzak of the woods but the messages and clues you are after. As you become sensitized to this way of listening, you will be surprised at what you have been missing. As with so many things, once you notice these sounds, you will hear them everywhere. Look for a yellow car on the highway, and soon you will notice hundreds of yellow cars. Once I heard my first red-winged blackbird of spring while driving a noisy dump truck. The sound of its call ("kong-a-ree") had managed to penetrate the rattle of the truck and my idle thoughts.

As you listen to what was once just background noise, you will want to match specific sounds to the right animals. Many people can point out a robin, but few can recognize its call ("cheerily-cheerily"). Many birds, however, have different calls for different activities, like staking out territory, scolding predators and mating.

Trees also can be told apart by the sounds they make

as the wind passes through their branches. Willows seem to whisper, pines sigh, locusts rustle as their big seed pods rub against each other. On a windy evening, these noises make up the night.

Some of the chatter in the forest will be from animals reporting on your movements. Bluejays, magpies and squirrels will reveal your location in the woods, as well as that of many predatory animals. If you keep alert you'll know if someone or something is moving through the woods. Hearing several birds or squirrels calling along a course is a reliable clue. If you hear these scolding animals behind you, someone or something is coming up the trail behind you.

Smell

In the Navy I served one stint on a destroyer escort in the Caribbean. One night I was on watch. I had been down below for five hours, and when I walked outside there was a lovely warm floral smell. It was striking. At sea the faintest scent stands out, because the smell of sea air is all there is and this serves as an empty canvas for the unusual. I looked around, but couldn't see anything because the superstructure was in the way. When I walked around it, there out in the distance was the light glow of an inhabited area. It was Martinique, a good 10 miles away. The wind was coming over the island and picking up the fragrance of everything that was growing there and bringing it out to sea.

On land we are confronted with many smells each day, most of which we take little note. Humans have a fairly good sense of smell, though not as good as many of the animals you will be stalking. You can sharpen your sense of smell by taking a little water and moistening your nostrils. Animals have wet noses to help them trap odors.

Water—as at sea—conveys smells. On a foggy, rainy night you'll smell things that on a dry night you would have missed.

Most of the time, we humans depend on our sense of sight, but we should learn to refine our sense of smell too. Tune into the subtlest scents, not just those aromas that hit you over the head. Make it a habit to stop in your daily routine and sniff the air. See if you can identify the smells.

You can follow your nose when you're afield. In the woods, I have located nearby fields by the smell of honeysuckle on a misty breeze, and farms by the smell of freshly plowed soil. The same sector of woods can smell entirely different from day to day. Since damp air is more fragrant than dry air, on a dry day I may not have smelled the honeysuckle.

Other plants give out odors as you step on them or brush against them. If they've been trampled, pennyroyals (*Hedeoma pulegioides*) release a minty smell that could penetrate most colds, and spice bush (*Lindera benzoin*) gives off a scent true to its name.

Of course, animals too have their odors. If you catch a scent in the air that reminds you of a wet dog, there may be a woodchuck, fox or other animal nearby. (Then again, it may be a wet dog.) Shallow breeding fish, especially bluegills, give off that distinct fishy smell when spawning.

You can't rely on your nose exclusively when in the woods, but when added to your heightened senses of sight and hearing, it will enhance your chances of spotting an animal and add a new accent to your experience of the woods.

On Spotting an Animal

Animals find us discomforting. They interpret our natural movements as threatening. Not walking on all fours, we tower over most creatures, which is viewed as a position of dominance, implying danger. We also stare. To an animal this is a sign that a predator is about to seize its prey. The animal will bolt. So, keep low and avoid a head-on gaze, averting your head to one side.

Your movements will communicate an intent to an animal. Often you can ease the animal's wariness by acting nonchalant, keeping your hands hidden and not held at chest level as if preparing to pounce.

Know the field of the animal's vision. Hawks see straight ahead and therefore are easier to move upon from behind. Rabbits and ducks, which have eyes set on the sides of their heads, have a wide range of vision.

The general rule is that predators have their eyes in front and prey have them on the side. Predators' stereoscopic vision, with its excellent depth perception, helps them to seize their prey. Most prey, always on the watch, benefit from a wide field of vision, having an eye on each side of the head. You must know how the animals sees to stalk it successfully.

Each kind of animal also has a sense of space, or spatial threshold, beyond which it will not let anyone approach. Crossing the invisible threshold line will cause it to flee. For example, small birds will let you get quite close, but many mammals will not let you within binocular range if they can help it.

The wariness of an individual animal also depends in part on the population of that species in the area. When a species has a low population, the animals are much more cautious than when there is a high population. This is called the "wariness cycle." When the population is low, each individual is under greater threat from predators. There are fewer eyes and ears on the lookout, and the odds are greater that any individual will be eaten. When the population is high, there is safety in numbers, and the threat of being killed is less. A higher population also forces an animal to be bolder in foraging for food, since competition for food increases.

Once you have spotted an animal, try to determine what the focus of its attention is. It may be feeding, drinking, nesting, or on the alert. This will determine how close you can get, and how to plan your pursuit. Move only when the animal is preoccupied. Try to time your movements to correspond with another source of noise, such as the wind blowing leaves or rattling tree branches or a bird calling. Move in quietly, using the stalking techniques discussed earlier. Try to keep your footsteps rhythmic.

If you make a noise, alerting your quarry to the presence of danger—freeze. Most wild animals won't recognize a motionless interloper. (Watch a cat or fox while stalking. They can freeze instantly, and hold that position with the immeasurable patience of all animals.)

Freezing in place will be easy if you are using the stalker's walk. No matter where you are in your stride, you should be able to comfortably become motionless without losing your balance or twisting yourself into a pretzel.

It is possible to change position while an animal is looking your way, but you must do it very slowly, with a flowing motion, as if slowed by molasses. This is quite difficult and will take some practice.

Usually, your quarry will look up if it hears a noise, and it will look about, trying to detect danger. After a short period, if not too spooked, it will return to its business. Wait until the animal is busy before resuming your stalk.

For instance, white-tailed deer are nervous animals. Even while feeding they are constantly looking about, keeping their heads down for only a few minutes at a time. These deer have keen eyesight. Do not move a muscle if they look your way. The deer's tail will tip you off. If the tail is all the way down, it is not suspicious, even though it may be looking toward you. If the tail moves up, short of a horizontal position, the deer is uneasy. It will probably move its head from side to side to get a better view. Stay still and it may return to feeding. If the tail is horizontal, the deer is edgy and will probably walk away. When the tail flips above the horizontal the deer is as good as gone. And a straight-up tail—looking like a floating white ostrich feather—will be the last you see of the deer.

If you have been spotted by an animal, there are a couple of last-ditch measures you can take. Try to make the animal think you haven't spotted it. Walk slowly on a course of travel that will take you past the animal at a distance far from its wariness threshold. If successful, the animal will freeze. But this technique won't fool very wary species.

You might also try sitting down. This will sometimes put a skittish animal at ease.

At times it may be necessary to drop—quietly—to the ground to avoid being spotted. First crouch down as silently as possible, feeling the ground for a place clear of twigs or leaves. Once you've found a clear spot, put your body's weight on the arm and hand that is already on the ground. Move the leg on that side of the body carefully backward. Next, plant the other hand on the ground and slowly extend the other leg. Then, as if coming down from a push up, lower the body gently to the ground.

When moving on your hands and knees, use your hands to clear a spot for your knee to come down upon. This will greatly reduce the amount of noise you'll make.

Drills

Rehearse your stalking in your backyard or a nearby park. Try stalking larger birds, such as geese, ducks and herons. This is difficult and your best bet is to move up on the bird while it is preening, sunning or feeding.

Frogs by the pond side are a tough test. Stalk along the bank, counting how many you can spot before they yelp and leap into the water. You'll be as startled as the frogs, and will not see most of them before they hit the water. But see how close you can get to the ones that are sitting still. These sensitive amphibians will help you judge your stalking skills. On a cold morning, however, you can practically jump up and down behind them before they'll move.

Around the house, the family dog is also a convenient target. See how close you can get to your loyal friend before it lifts up its head to look at you with puzzlement. Cats, squirrels and many other small animals can be stalked in this fashion.

2

TRACKING

Crossroads in the Woods

An animal's tracks are a diary left in soil and snow. Naturalists are skilled readers of these diaries. John K. Terres, in *From Laurel Hill to Siler's Bog: The Walking Adventures of a Naturalist*, tells of following the trail of two gray foxes across a North Carolina farm. The tracks had been left the night before in wet snow. They were, he says, "etched in the snow as sharply as that of a small dog in wet concrete." Terres, following the trail over 5 miles, was able to recreate the nocturnal trip of the foxes—a male and a female, he judged by the track size.

He saw how they walked side by side, with exact fox footing, "as if only one paw had touched the snow" in each trail; where they had run wildly, playfully; where they had stopped to scent the snow with urine.

At the edge of an oak woods, the two foxes had parted to hunt. He followed what he believed to be the male. He could see where the fox had slowed his pace at the honeysuckle thicket, then turned and leapt, kicking up the snow and the leaves underneath, chasing the bounding tracks of a rabbit, and then gave up and resumed his

23

travels; scratched the snow under a white oak for acorns,
leaving behind crunched bits; traveled on, southward, into
the scent-bringing wind; jumped over a log, leaving behind
spots of blood from a woodland mouse he had eaten; and
went on, circling eastward, stalking a flock of wild turkeys—crouching from thicket to thicket, creeping behind
a tree, then leaving deep marks in the snow, as it pounced
at 35 miles an hour or so after the turkeys—tracks, long
strides, wing marks, the turkeys were off. Terres could see
where they had alighted hundreds of yards away to resume
feeding.

He followed the fox's trail through a swamp, in narrow
passage between the sweet gum trees (almost losing the
trail where the fox had run up a sycamore and jumped
down, breaking the scent trail), then over a log across a
stream where Terres was rewarded with the discovery of
the foxes' den in the hollow trunk of a fallen willow. The
tracks of the female rejoined the male there.

An entire story of a night's journey, read in the tracks.
In the end, Terres had learned more about the foxes than
he had from many glimpses of the "ghosts slipping into the
shadows of the woods trails without a whisper of sound."

Terres is an experienced reader of natural signs, but
by knowing what to look for, the woods will seem busy with
the crossroads of voles, the stichings of mouse trails in the
snow, the double-hop track of the squirrel and the tripod
stand of the rabbit. Opossum, skunk and raccoon tracks
are the next easiest to recognize. These animals have
distinctive tracks and a limited territory.

By traveling the same paths every day, you'll soon
develop a fairly accurate census of the wildlife in your area.
And you'll develop a profile of the animal you are following,
much the way Terres followed the fox.

Keep in mind the kind of animals you are likely to find
in your area. Don't expect the exotic. A friend insisted that
a certain set of tracks we were following belonged to the

small-clawed Oriental otter—admittedly a bit out of its range in New Hampshire—rather than what it was in fact: the big-clawed neighborhood Labrador retriever.

Time of Day

It is easiest to track when the sun is low on the horizon—early morning or late afternoon—casting long shadows, which give the tracks sharp relief. Noon is the most difficult time to track. Try to keep the track between yourself and the sun.

Proceed in a "connect-the-dots" fashion. Don't pass any one track until you have located the next one. Read the trail ahead before you move on, being careful not to destroy any of the tracks or other animal signs. Mark the last sign or track you found so you can return to it. Make a mark in the soil or put a pebble where the last track is.

Combine a close examination of the trail with a long scan down the trail. Don't hesitate to get down on your hands and knees for a look around, at times resting one ear against the ground, looking toward where the next track should be. If the track is still hard to see, squint through one eye, then the other. Faint tracks on hard-packed ground show up this way. At other times, a look down the trail will reveal the pattern of travel.

The Tracks

No two animals leave the same track. Some may be close, but with practice you can tell them apart. There are clues in the paw print and in the pattern of tracks.

The toes are the first clue. Find a clear track and count the number of toe marks. This will reduce the number of animals the tracks could belong to. Wild animals can be categorized by their toe marks as follows:

1. hoofed (two-toed, half-moon-like tracks): white-tailed deer, moose, cows;
2. four toes, front and hind: foxes, dogs, cats, rabbits;
3. five toes, front and hind: weasels, skunks, opossums, muskrats, raccoons, beavers; and
4. four toes front, five toes hind: most rodents; squirrels, mice, chipmunks, woodchucks.

Be sure you have a good print, with all toes showing, otherwise you can be misled.

While looking at the paw print, see if there are any claw marks. This is a further clue. For example, cats and foxes leave behind trails that are quite similar, but cats walk with claws retracted, foxes with claws out. Also notice the shape of the track. Both opossums and skunks have five toes on all feet and show claw marks, but their tracks have entirely different shapes. In the final chapter, the tracks of thirty wide-ranging North American animals are identified individually.

Gaits

Often, before you have a good look at an individual track print, you will have noticed the pattern of tracks. These reveal the way an animal walks, its gait. There are four basic gaits: walk, bound, gallop and pace.

Dogs, cats and hoofed animals use a walking gait. They move opposing limbs at the same time: the left front foot advances with the right rear foot, then the right front foot comes forward with the left rear foot, much like a baby's crawl.

All cats, foxes and deer, as well as some other animals, walk in register, putting their hind feet exactly where their forefeet have been. This is an excellent step for silent walking

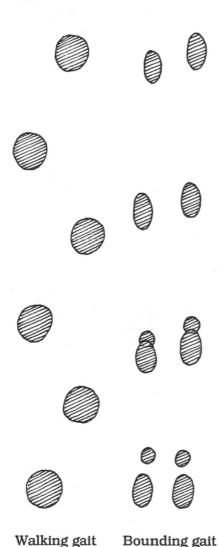

Walking gait   Bounding gait

(and is the model for the stalker's walk discussed earlier). Domestic dogs, wolves and coyotes all leave their rear prints a little behind and to the side of the front feet. They walk out of register, but occasionally the prints will overlap.

Weasels and a few other animals with long bodies and short legs move by bounding. The front feet come forward together and the back feet, moving together, land close behind. They jump or bound forward with their bodies moving in an S-shaped wave. From the side, they seem to move with a cartoon-like skittering motion. They leave behind prints in rectangular formation, a paw in each corner.

All rabbits and rodents, except some wide-bodied species like muskrats and beavers, move at a gallop or hop. These animals push off with their back feet, landing on both their front feet, as both their hind feet continue forward to rest ahead of their front feet. The wide-bodied beaver, muskrat and porcupine will gallop or bound only if they need speed.

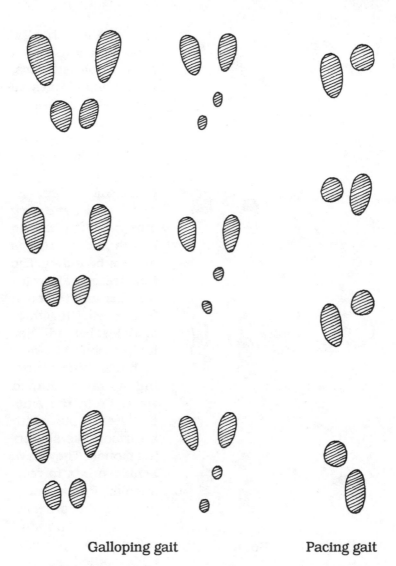

Galloping gait   Pacing gait

If the front feet of a galloping animal hit the ground side by side, it's a good indication that the animal making the track is a tree dweller, such as a squirrel. If the feet land diagonally, the animal is likely to be a ground dweller such as a rabbit.

Most wide-bodied animals do a good deal of pacing. This is the walk that gives the raccoon its characteristic lumbering gait. One side of the body is moved at a time— left front, left rear, then right front, right rear. Due to the wide backs of these animals, raccoons and others will seem to roll as they walk, side to side, as if they were shipboard. Bears, opossums, muskrats, skunks, beavers and porcupines will also pace.

Pacing animals and those that walk on the diagonal change their gaits as they speed up; a dog on the run leaves a different pattern of tracks than one walking. But bounders and gallopers just increase the distance between the points where their feet touch the ground; the weasel, for instance, leaves behind longer rectangles of prints.

Once you learn the basic gaits, you'll recognize these variations as you go along. The individual print itself can tell you whether the animal is on the move: when running or trotting in sand, soft earth or snow, the landing feet will push up a small ridge forward of the track, and may also kick out a plume of dirt behind.

Two other measures help to identify tracks. One is the trail width, which is the distance between the outermost points of a set of right and left prints. This gives a measure of how wide the animal is. The other is stride, the distance between one track or a set of tracks and the next. This gives an idea of the length of the animal, letting you know how it moves with each step. This, too, like its gait, varies with the speed of the animal.

The stride of the animal can be measured with a walking stick. Measure the distance from the heel of one track to the next by putting the end of the stick in one heelmark, noting where the previous heelmark intersects with the stick. Use a rubber band to mark this distance and you now have the measure of the animal's stride. If you lose the track, place the rubber band marker on the stick in the heelmark of the last track and extend your stick down the trail. The next track will be at the end of the stick.

Besides hoof or paw prints, several animals drag their tails along—opossums, muskrats, beavers—and these trail marks can help identify the animal. (A New York friend claims to have seen the tail drags of sewer rats in the slush of Eighth Avenue.)

What we have been doing here is constructing an animal from the ground up. From toe and claw, to forelegs and hindlegs, and on to the stride and gait, which leads up to the animal's body and its motion, and starts to tell us what it is, and perhaps, what the animal is up to.

Best Tracking Conditions

Think back a moment to the world Terres awoke to on his farm the morning he followed the foxes. Snow, wet snow at that, the type of day that makes "a naturalist feel lucky," as he said. A good snow leaves the landscape new. It's a clean slate.

For first-time trackers, as well, these are the best days to begin; after a snow, a heavy rain or a windstorm has wiped the land clear. The animals, denned up during a storm, will be out looking for food. All the tracks will be fresh, with sharp edges.

The lightest footfall will leave a good track in snow. However, loose, powdery snow is a problem. It drifts into tracks, making identification difficult. Snow that is crusted over may allow lighter animals to pass without leaving a track. Wet snow takes the best footprint, and these prints will remain fresh for several hours or days when the temperature is below freezing and the snow is not drifting.

As time passes, the sharp edges of tracks will begin to round off, the soil or snow at the edge of the print falling in. Tracks will become eroded by rain drops, melted by sun, covered over by the wind. Taking into account the type of sand or soil, the terrain and the weather, you can get a sense of the age of the tracks from such observations.

It's difficult to tell how old a track in sand might be, but a fresh track will generally look darker than the surrounding sand because the moisture below the surface has been exposed. Other surfaces are more deceptive: wet clay can dry out and leave fresh-looking tracks for weeks. Many of the dinosaur tracks seen as fossils in museums were laid down in similar conditions. Dry tracks in clay mud are likely old tracks. If the surface is dry you will probably have to work at leaving a scuff mark, so don't expect a light-footed, lightweight animal to make deep prints.

To best gauge the age of tracks in any soil, use your own tracks as a guide, using the sharpness and color of your print for comparison. When estimating the time the tracks were made check out several different areas, because they age at different rates. For example, if tracks are sheltered under pine trees, in thickets or behind rocks, they will last longer than those out in the open. When following an old trail, look for these sheltered places, where you may be able to fill in the details of tracks. (Conversely, tracks by roads and parking lots may be younger than they seem at first glance, since they have had much dirt an dust thrown in them.)

When the snow melts as it warms up, tracks tend to enlarge and spread out. They will metamorphose into distorted monster versions of the animal: raccoon tracks the size of a dog, human tracks that resemble a race of Brobdingnagians.

Signs

Along with tracks, animals leave other signs of their travels. They rearrange the furniture just a bit, kicking up rocks, breaking branches, matting down vegetation. In

high grass, they leave a trail of parted grasses. In the
woods, there will be broken twigs, which show brighter at
the break, and overturned leaves with their damp undersides facing upwards. The moss on exposed roots and
rocks may be scuffed off. A low branch, a briar patch or
barbed wire may snag the animal, grasping bits of fur.
Skunks, I have found, always seem to be leaving bits of
their pelt around.

If there is a soft and thick bed of leaves, the track will
show as a series of depressions or scuff marks in the
leaves. On harder ground, pebbles will be kicked up from
their beds, a wet soiled side showing. Other pebbles will be
moved only slightly, showing a rim of wet underside. At
other times, the pebble will be pressed harder into the soil,
due to a foot, paw or hoof stepping directly on it, leaving a
rim of soil up around the rock, or a gap in the soil where
the pebble has been shifted by the weight of the padding
animal.

Some signs tell you that nothing has passed that way.
Cobwebs across a path or burrow entrance. Or a dry turtle:
a turtle with a dry shell resting near shore is a good sign
that it has not felt the need to move for at least ten to fifteen
minutes.

Losing the Trail

Even with all the signs and tracks about, still there
are no arrows, no display cards ("Porcupine Next 1,000
Feet"). It is easy to lose the trail you are trying to follow.

One of the most common places to lose a trail is where
an animal changes direction—the trail abruptly ends. If
the stride measurer on your walking stick fails to reveal a
track, stop at the last track you have found and look
around the area, scanning in a widening circle. If this fails,
backtrack a short way to see if the animal itself has not

backtracked and jumped off the trail. If this doesn't work, go back to the last track and walk in ever-widening circles until you come across the trail.

While looking around for a track, ask yourself the old question: "Now where would I go if I were a ... ?" Note the terrain, look for worn paths, broken twigs, obvious places of travel. Many trails converge at favored feeding areas and watering holes. (The shores of streams, rivers and lakes are always good places to look for tracks.) Some old trails will be worn into the earth from generations of habitual use.

Sometimes the animal may have gone into a tangle of brush. Walk around the brush to see if you can find the tracks coming out. Don't be surprised if the animal bolts from the brush just as you round that side.

After spotting an animal, observe the track it just left. This is the best way to learn to recognize animal tracks.

Along the shore, animals may break trail by jumping into the water. Walk along watching for the tracks to emerge. While the animal may have crossed to the other side, often these animals—raccoons, muskrats—just dip into the water and come out again. This technique of walking an area in hopes of picking up the trail again is called "cutting sign" by experienced trackers. It is more reassuring to tell yourself that you are "cutting sign" rather than lost or a mite bewildered.

If you can't find the trail, you can turn around and backtrack, following the animal's journey to its source.

But if the trail is lost for the day, don't despair. You now know a little bit about the animal, and since most animals travel fixed routes in small areas, you'll likely cross paths again.

3

BIRDS

The Landscape of Sound

The surrounding countryside is a mystery, as curious and secretive as it used to be rendered in the fairy tales of a more enchanted age. Here are some possible scenarios.

Walking about, you come across a bird in apparent distress. It cries out. It wobbles around with a broken wing and seems to be in its death throes, breathing erratically and finally rolling over. Above the ailing bird, another circles, crying out. A poisoned bird? An odd courtship? What you have witnessed is a drama, though you lack the script. It is the female killdeer distracting you, trying to lure you away from her nest, with the help of the male overhead.

Or consider this riddle. At the edge of a clearing, in a tree, you come upon what at first glance looks like a moss-covered walnut. Inside it is hollow, and on careful examination it seems to have been sewn together with silk, like that from a caterpillar nest or spider web. The inside hollow is lined with milkweed or thistle and young oak leaves. Is this a spider's home or an elaborate cocoon? No. It's the nest of a ruby-throated hummingbird.

These are mysteries of identification, woodland side-
shows. But there are many other intriguing questions—
most without an answer. For example, over 200 species of
birds—robins and blue jays included—are known to put
live or crushed ants on their feathers; some theorize that
the birds are grooming or are trying to rid themselves of
parasites, but there are no real answers. Or, how is it that
entire flocks of birds, such as starlings, can turn as a single
entity without the birds in the rear bumping into those up
front? Another curiosity: cedar waxwings perched in a row
pass morsels of food up and down the line from one bird's
bill to the other. Of course, the greatest of all bird mysteries
is how they fly thousands of miles, across continents,
across oceans, to arrive home in your backyard. Again
there are no real answers, but there are many ideas,
theories and much research. The woods and fields are
littered with mysteries.

This chapter concerns itself with learning about some
of the comings and goings of the birds in your area. There
are clues all over: nests, songs, distinctive behaviors. By
working from these signs you can identify the birds. This
is a different approach from using a field guide, in which
you start with a good idea of what you're seeing. In a sense,
this chapter is a preliminary to a field guide. It's about
discovering the hidden patterns; a field guide will fine-tune
your findings. Everything discussed here should be possible to see within a season or two of looking. Robins, crows
and chickadees, just to mention a few, lead pretty interest-
ing lives.

On Going Forth

The early morning hours, after first light, are best for
bird-watching (remember the early bird). In summer, 4:30
A.M. is not too early to start. Birds are best observed with

the sun at your back. This way you can clearly see the bird's color and markings. If the bird is between you and the sun, all you will see is a dark silhouette. By walking west in the morning and east in the evening, the sun will be at your back.

A slow stroll is the best way of trying to get close to birds. Here, stalking will not be effective. (A bird's eyesight can be forty times better than a human's.) Once you're within good distance of a bird, freeze. If you have field glasses, bring them up to your eyes slowly. It's best to remain quiet, but if you talk, keep in mind that birds with low-pitched voices are more sensitive to low-pitched sounds, and those with high-pitched song are sensitive to high-pitched sound. If you know a bird's call, speak in the opposite pitch. A whisper may be more noticeable to some species than normal conversation.

As you observe a bird there are three things to look for immediately: size, location and behavior. Is the bird bigger than a crow? Robin-sized? Where did you see it—on the ground, in a tree, soaring? And what about its behavior? Pecking a tree, diving into a stream, or darting out from a lofty perch to catch flying insects? Then you move on to scanning the markings on the bird itself or trying to identify its nest.

Many bird species are confined to specialized habitats, and this is an excellent way to identify them. The field sparrow and the swamp sparrow are two 5-inch birds with mottled brown backs, light undersides and rust-colored caps on their heads. They live in the same region but in different habitats. The field sparrow is found in abandoned fields and pastures, while the swamp sparrow, true to its name, is found in marshes and bogs.

Listening for Birds

You will find far more birds by using your ears instead of your eyes. In many cases, the bird songs are the landscape made aural. Songs are a report of clearings in the woods, water nearby, the light on the land. The pitch of a bird song can tell you where to look. Higher pitched songs tend to come from birds that sing from a higher perch. Low-pitched sounds are affected less by objects in their path, so the lower pitched birds tend to sing on the ground.

This distinction in pitch is observable even in birds of similar families. In the warbler family, oven birds and the Kentucky warbler, which sing from the ground, have lower pitched songs than those of the Blackpoll and Blackburnian warbler, which sing in trees.

To attract a mate, birds that sing from well-concealed areas must produce sounds that are easily located. Their songs may buzz and rattle and repeat: the "krawk-kok" of a pheasant in a cornfield and the "kut-kut churrrrrr-ur" of the long-billed marsh wren. These rattling calls are more easily pinned down than pure tones, like high thin whistles.

In the open country of meadows and prairies, birds sing from a point above the ground that gives a good view of the territory and helps their call to carry. Meadowlarks and sparrows living in the grassland habitats will sing from the few trees, bushes and fences in the area. They have regular song perches.

In open areas, many birds, such as the bobolink, horned lark, upland plover and skylark, sing while in flight. This allows their song to carry far and is often accompanied by spiraling courtship flights.

Listening for the songs of the bobolink, killdeer, meadowlark and goldfinch can lead you to open places in the woods. If you hear several meadowlarks, you are near a tall grass meadow. The sound of red-winged blackbirds calling is a sign of water nearby. And the call of the American bittern ("oong-ka-chunk") will lead you to a marsh or a pond lined with reeds.

Birds sing from preferred spots or favorite song perches. Most song birds sing from branches or hidden places near the ground. Song perches need not be very high—fence posts, low shrubs or even the top of a weed for some birds. While robins may sing from the ground, usually they sing at a height of 12 feet or more. The robin is a good bird to look for. By knowing the area where a handful of common birds sing you will have a system for scouting them out. You won't have to start by looking at everything in the area, your head swiveling this way and that.

If you hear a mockingbird call, you should look at the top of every prominent object in the area—roofs, trees, flag poles. Blue-winged warblers also sing from exposed perches high up in bushes and trees.

Thrushes, in general, are secretive. They live in the woods and are hard to spot. Once you've found the tree their song is coming from, look near the trunk; they almost always perch on a thick limb within a foot or two of the trunk. The main exceptions to this rule about thrushes are the robin and bluebird.

There are several other common calls, so frequently heard they are part of the daily noise we shut out.

Crows have a number of calls. The one to listen for is the mobbing call. This is a rapid sequence of "caws" that I've come to realize means the crows have found an owl or hawk and are harrying it. This call has led to most of the owls I've seen.

Chickadees, as well, have a large repertoire. "Dee dee dee" is the call of a dominant bird asserting its place in the pecking order. "Tseet tseeet" is the call it uses to keep its flock together when feeding in dense growth. If a bird has strayed and lost track of the flock, it will call out its name, "chick a dee."

Blue jays frequently seem to use ventriloquism. Sometimes they can stay in one spot and make it seem as if their
call is coming first from far off, then from nearby. Unlike
most birds that fall silent when other animals invade their
territory, the blue jay will loudly scold the intruders.

At times they use their alarm call to clear out other
birds at a feeder. I have been told blue jays sometimes
imitate the screams of certain hawks to clear the way, but
I have never seen it done.

Bird Songs

A wave of song moves across the continent each
morning, east to west, with sunrise. Light—a certain
intensity of light—starts birds singing.

As the days lengthen, birds begin singing earlier each
morning. A cloudy day will delay singing. A bright, full
moon can start many species singing earlier, particularly
robins. As the light dims in the evening, the songs trail off.
This relationship of light and song is reversed for nocturnal
birds, like nighthawks. They sing at dusk, stopping at
dawn.

In general, the earliest birds to start singing are those
that feed on insects, followed by seed-eating species and,
last, birds that live in tree holes.

Robins begin singing in the faint morning sun, while
many other birds await more light. Robins stop singing in
the afternoon unless it's cloudy, and begin again at dusk,
with a quieter evening song. This is a pattern that most
daytime birds follow. However, early in spring, during the
mating season, many are likely to call through the day.

You are more likely to hear a male wild turkey gobble
in the morning than in the late afternoon. They are most
vocal in the spring when calling for females. Some birds
that sing from perches or on the ground during the day,

such as the ovenbird, sing different flight songs in the evening.

A few birds will sing all day through: mockingbirds, wrens and vireos. Mockingbirds will sing all night, too, particularly if the moon is full. The vesper sparrow sings one hour after sunset, at vespers—except during nesting season, when it sings all day. The eastern wood pewee will be singing before sunrise.

By July the countryside will be much quieter. Most birds have finished mating and territories have been defined.

Calling Birds

Most bird calls are difficult to learn and require not only the duplication of their sound but also of how the sounds are linked together. It's tricky to put down on paper what the calls sound like, and describing them to another person is often an occasion for very silly conversation. It is as if everything was suddenly reduced to a Pidgin English tapped out in Morse code. However, there are several species of birds whose calls can be easily imitated to draw them in closer.

Bobwhites sing their names in two notes (one long, one short), sometimes ending with a three-note call that sounds like "poor bobwhite." A kitten-like "mew" may attract a catbird. The whistled "old-sam-peabody" call of the white-throated sparrow and the "wheat-wheat-wheat" call of the cardinal can be imitated.

The titmouse sings a clear, clean whistle of three notes, run together, "peter-peter-peter," and run closer together, "peer-peer-peer," resembling the notes of the cardinal. The bird almost always responds to this call, coming forward to look around.

You can bring other birds closer by imitating the

territorial calls of males, in particular. This works well, I've found, with northern orioles, white-throated sparrows, rose-breasted grosbeaks and screech and great horned owls.

Some birds will respond to imitations of different species. Often, just before dusk, you can get wild turkeys to gobble by imitating the hoot of an owl. And, if your owl hoots are good enough, you can call in some crows. Some "birders" (that dedicated bunch of bird-watchers) imitate the whinnying call of the screech owl to flush birds from cover.

Other Bird Sounds

During the months of summer and autumn, what began so musically in the spring ends as a whisper. Some birds sing a melancholy whisper song. They sing their regular songs with their beaks closed, or very quietly from cover in trees, and you're not likely to notice these songs unless you happen upon them. American goldfinches and rose-breasted grosbeaks sing these plaintive calls while sitting on a nest. Brown thrashers, evening grosbeaks and catbirds also are known to have this song.

Another frequently heard sound is made by woodpeckers as they drill into trees. Each species of woodpecker makes a specific hammering sound. The large pileated woodpecker hammers out twelve strokes on average, rising in frequency toward the middle, and trailing away. The hairy woodpecker, a robin-sized bird, is more hesitant, pecking at trees with short, well-paced taps. The downy woodpecker has a longer sequence of taps, drumming against the tree with rapid strokes that sound muted. Woodpeckers drum upon especially resonant trees in their territories to attract mates.

The ruffed grouse also drums. In the spring, the male climbs a rock or log and drums the air with its wings. It starts slowly, making hollow thumping sounds, then speeds up, sounding like a whir. With favorable wind conditions, the grouse's drumming can be heard for over a mile, but it is a sound that is hard to locate.

Bird Nests

If you ask a class of grade-school kids to place a bird's nest in a standard lollipop tree, most will draw in the nest in the tree tops, "close to heaven." And many adults would concur. But the top of a tree catches all the weather and sways in breezes of only 10 miles per hour; in a storm, a nest would be like a sea-tossed fishing boat, so most birds nest lower down. A study of nesting sites in a wooded area near Pittsburgh showed that more than one-third of all nests were less than 2 feet above ground. Half the nests were lower than 6 feet, and only eight nests out of several hundred were found higher than 35 feet.

Most bird nests tend to be below 10 feet in open woodland with lower brush and in open brushy fields. In an older forest, however, with only tall trees, nests are commonly located higher up.

The best times to find bird nests are when the birds are building them, or when they're bringing food to their young; at these times birds make many trips and take less notice of humans. If you are familiar with bird calls, listen for the territorial song of the male. This will tell you that there is a bird nest in the area.

Nests are usually very well hidden, but if you go through a familiar field in winter, after a snowfall, the bird nests will stand out in relief, like snow-piled platforms. Bird nests will appear to be plentiful, yet in summer you might have seen only a fraction of them.

A bird's feeding area is not necessarily its nesting site. Mourning doves, normally found feeding in open fields and lawns, nest in the brush and trees of the open woods and orchards, and often in the lower branches of evergreen trees.

Birds that nest early sometimes don't build their first nests in the same place as their later ones. The song sparrow may nest first on the ground, and later in the bushes. The American robin often puts its first nest in an evergreen and a later one in a deciduous tree. In both cases, the birds choose alternate nest sites because of the lack of leaves on trees and shrubs in early spring.

To identify a nest, consider the nest's construction: where it is located, its size and shape and the materials used.

Robins prefer to nest in tree forks or on horizontal branches, usually 5 to 15 feet above ground. But they will also use shrubs and ledges. The cup-shaped nest is 6 to 7 inches across, made of grasses, twigs, string and paper mixed together with mud.

This mud is so important to the robin that, if none is around, the bird will make some by dipping its feet in water and then standing on dry earth. (Barn swallows also produce mud this way.) The mud is used as the mortar of the nest. The robin sits inside the nest, rotating on its stomach to sculpt the right shape. The mud is then covered with softer plants. (The wood thrush, a close relative of the robin, builds a similar, smaller nest, but it has leaves in the foundation.) The robin does such a good job that its abandoned nests are sometimes taken over by the mourning dove, whose own nest is a platform of twigs so thinly constructed that the egg can be seen from below.

Vireos make small nests, suspended by the rim from branches or twigs. The nest is open at the top, no larger than 3 1/2 inches across and only 2 inches deep. It is constructed of woven plant fibers, spider silk, plant down, rootlets and paper from old hornets' nests, the exact mix depending on the species of vireo.

Sparrows (song, chipping and field sparrows) make small, cup-shaped nests of neatly formed grass. Sometimes they are lined with horse hair or fishing line (birds are great improvisers) and are built low to the ground, usually less than 3 feet. Some may be on the ground itself.

Small nests of soft milkweed or thistledown and grasses are often built in the crotches of sapling trees by yellow warblers, goldfinches, flycatchers and redstarts. The downy materials show as white or gray in the nest's foundation, but rain and weathering make these distinguishing characteristics less clear.

The ruby-throated hummingbird makes the smallest of nests, 1 inch deep by 1 inch wide. Sometimes they'll nest on a tiny twig. The nest is usually at the edge of a wooded area or clearing, about 5 to 20 feet above the ground. The upper edge of the thin nest curves in to protect the two bean-sized eggs. The walls of the nest are made from the down of several species of plants and young oak leaves, woven into place with silk from spiderwebs or cocoons. The outside is camouflaged with moss and lichen.

Unlike other birds, the hummingbird doesn't hide its nest but places it near the tips of branches. Nonetheless, the hummingbird's nest is very hard to find.

Northern orioles also build nests hanging from the tips of branches, usually willows, elms and maples. I often notice these in the fall, hanging over a road. Their distinctive shape is hard to miss. The nests are located about 25 to 30 feet above ground and are 5 to 9 inches tall. Woven from yarn, plant fiber and hairs, they are a gray color.

On vertical surfaces or high ledges look for nests of the barn or cliff swallow and eastern phoebe. The barn swallow builds a cone-shaped nest of mud reinforced with grass or straw and lined with feathers. On a flat surface, the nest will be cup-shaped. The eastern phoebe builds in similar locations, but its nests are moss covered and lined with finer grass or hair. The cliff swallow builds a gourd-

shaped nest made of clay pellets and lined with feathers.
    Woodpeckers can be roughly identified by the size of
the holes they make:

downy	1 1/2 inches diameter
red-headed	2 inches diameter
hairy	2 1/2 inches diameter
yellow-shafted flicker	2–4 inches diameter
pileated	3 1/2–4 1/2 inches diameter

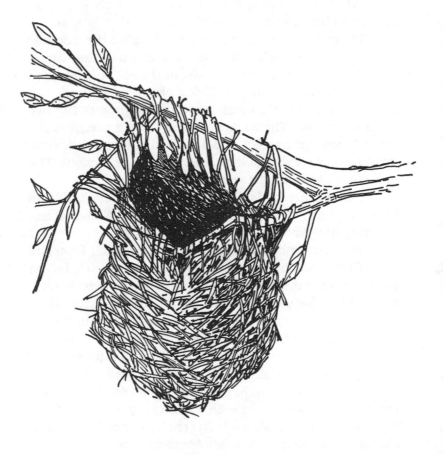

Oriole nest

The hairy woodpecker and the downy woodpecker are quite similar. But the hairy woodpecker prefers the dead branches of live trees and makes holes that are slightly taller than they are round; the downy makes perfectly round holes and prefers to nest in dead trees. The birds look similar, but if you see the two species together, you'll notice the downy's bill is much shorter. The hairy woodpecker's bill is as long as its head. The male of both species has red on the back of its head; the females aren't so marked.

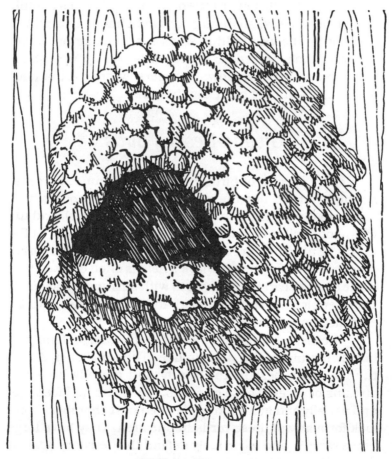

Cliff swallow nest

Most of the smaller woodpeckers' nest holes are on the east and south sides of trees, under the lower side of branches or sloping trunks. This lets in the warm morning sun and keeps the rain out.

The crow-sized pileated woodpecker makes large oval or rectangular holes in trees, leaving piles of wood chunks at the tree's base.

Woodpeckers aren't the only birds that peck holes in trees. Nuthatches, titmice and chickadees dig out holes for nests in trees with soft or rotten wood. Chickadees usually choose dead trees, such as gray birch, and are careful to carry away the wood chips so as not to make predators aware of their presence. Some birds will occupy abandoned holes—tree swallows, creepers, wrens, nuthatches and titmice—if they can't dig their own.

Ground Nesting Birds

Many species of birds nest on the ground. Some do not build a nest, like the nighthawk, which chooses bare fields or gravelly areas (and sometimes flat roofs), and the whip-poor-will, which lays its eggs on the leafy floor of the woods. But other ground layers make more elaborate preparations. The meadowlark's nest is often covered by a dome of grass carefully woven in with surrounding plants. The ovenbird also builds a leaf and grass dome, with an entrance on one side.

The belted kingfisher belongs to a large family of burrowing birds, the Alcedinidae. The kingfisher digs a tunnel for its nest in the sandy and gravelly banks of streams or lakes. These burrows may be up to 7 feet long and usually end in a slightly elevated nest chamber. Don't look for many of these birds in one area. They have large home ranges, and vigorously defend this territory against others of their kind.

Nestlings

The nesting period for many species is short. Robins leave the nest fourteen days or so after hatching. Killdeer, pheasant, quail and many waterfowl leave the nest after only a few days to hunt for food with parents.

But don't look for eggshells piling up under nests as a sign of newborns. Birds eat these shells or remove them, carrying them away some distance to avoid attracting predators and parasites. Sometimes adult birds will fit the small part of the shell into the larger part and drop it on the ground away from the nest. For some time, these packed pieces of eggshell were a mystery to me.

Some authorities claim they can tell the fate of the egg by examining the discarded shell: if the bird has hatched, there will be a small flap of dried membrane tissue along the inside edge of the break in the shell; an egg that has been eaten by a predator will not show that flap, but part of the yolk or white will be evident inside. Others disagree and say the female will sometimes clean out the hatched shell herself.

Birds have been known to mount spirited defenses of their nests. Robins have attacked squirrels, hummingbirds have attacked eagles (not such an uneven match when you consider the hummingbird's pointed beak and hovering ability) and ptarmigan have attacked grizzly bears. Blue jays, gray catbirds, mockingbirds, gulls, hawks and rails, to name a few, have been known to attack humans that they felt were threatening their young. No matter how peaceful your intentions, there's always a chance that you'll be seen as a threat.

Another defense, used by killdeers and ovenbirds, is to distract intruders from the ground nest. Walking along, you may suddenly find an adult bird in front of you acting as if it is crippled, stumbling and dragging one of its wings.

Once you've been lured away from the nest, it will leap into the air and fly off. If you persist and look around for a patch of open, stony or gravelly ground, you can usually find the eggs: buff-colored, mottled with dark brown blotches, camouflaged.

Feeding and Roosting

One or two hours before sunset, I have seen thousands of starlings in flocks extending several miles, flying to a nearby city to roost on the buildings. Starling roosts may comprise over 100,000 birds. When they get to their site, they begin singing, as if in celebration. Starlings will use roost locations for several years, as many plagued towns know. The droppings will kill anything growing below.

In the winter, crows break into small groups to forage during the day, but gather into roosts near dusk. Most of the roosts I have seen comprise well over 1,000 birds, but up to 10,000 cawing crows can roost in one area, covering the trees. When you see a group of crows feeding, look around and you are sure to spot one up in a tree or at another vantage point acting as a lookout, ready to give an alarm call. Blackbirds also gather in flocks to feed. They occupy and move across a field in a way that is notable, with the birds at the rear of the flock flying over the leading edge and landing in front of them. At times, it looks like a rolling hoop of birds moving across the clearing.

Why do blackbirds, crows and starlings flock and roost together? The theory is that there is safety in numbers—more eyes to watch predators—and short-lived food supplies like berries and insect swarms can be exploited more effectively.

Even for the most bird-blinded among us, it's hard to miss a thousand or more birds feeding. But spotting certain other birds takes a closer look. Most birds forage in a loose, scattered fashion—especially ground feeders like sparrows, thrushes, catbirds and finches, or tree feeders like woodpeckers, nuthatches and sapsuckers.

A good way to remember where a bird is likely to feed is to take note of its beak. Each is adapted to its function. Cardinals and grosbeaks are seed eaters; they have strong beaks for crushing seeds. Ducks have flattened bills to strain food from water. The creeper has a thin, curved probe for picking insects out of bark. The woodpecker's beak is a sharp chisel. The hawk is a flesh-eater; its hooked, curved beak, akin to a can opener, rips into prey. The long, straight beak like that of many shore and marsh birds is used for probing shallow waters and muddy bottoms.

Woodpeckers, nuthatches and creepers search the trunks of trees and large branches for food. Woodpeckers and creepers fly from the top of one tree to the base of the next and begin working their way up the trunk. Brown creepers take a spiralling, barbershop-pole course up the tree. Woodpeckers take a much straighter route, sometimes searching only one side of a trunk. Woodpeckers will also back down a tree, using their stiff tail feathers for support. (Creepers never do this.)

If you see a bird climbing down a tree head first it is probably a nuthatch, which can climb either up or down; this allows them to spot insects missed by other birds. Arriving at the bottom of a tree, they'll fly off to the top of the next tree. Creepers and woodpeckers work from the bottom up.

Red-headed woodpeckers and white-breasted nuthatches will sometimes wedge nuts into the crevices of a tree, and then drill through the nut's shell to get at the meat. These woodpeckers will often use the same crevice over and over, while the nuthatch keeps moving about the tree, storing nuts here and there. The white-breasted nuthatch, along with titmice and others, will also store sunflower seeds in crevices. Red-headed woodpeckers will store acorns and beechnuts in the cracks of fence posts and telephone poles as well as in dead trees.

Yellow-bellied sapsuckers tap trees for sap, leaving lines of close, evenly spaced borings on the tree. They return regularly to feed on the sap from these holes and the insects that become trapped there. This is a good place to watch for hummingbirds and animals like squirrels, which are drawn to the sap. Hummingbirds can sometimes be seen following a sapsucker to find freshly drilled holes.

Chickadees are noted tree feeders whose activities, once you learn them, will stand out in the woods like a fluorescent stripe on a tree. Chickadees have the amazing ability to hang upside down on small branches while feeding on insects, seeds and fruit. Perhaps this gives them a better chance at insect eggs and larvae. In the winter, chickadees will be out in the worst of midwinter storms, hanging upside down to get at seeds and cones not covered by snow.

Pigeons and doves are unique among birds in that they can drink with their heads down. Other birds have to get a mouthful of water and then tilt their heads back.

Hawks, Owls and Crows: Scattered Clues

Falcons, hawks, owls and crows leave clues to their presence scattered on the forest floor: regurgitated pellets composed of undigested parts of their prey. Being at the top of the food chain, they don't need to worry about leaving traces of their whereabouts.

Owl pellets look like matted felt with bits of bone showing through. They are usually found at the base of the owl's roosting place and vary with the size of the owl. Look up and you may see the owl roosting. Wildlife biologists study these pellets of fur, feathers and bones to determine the owl's diet and its species.

The barn owl's pellets tend to be black and somewhat shiny. Composed of fur and bones of small mammals, or feathers and bones of small birds, the barn owl's pellets have rounded ends and measure about 2 inches by 1 inch. They are found under large trees or buildings in quiet environments. The barred owl leaves pellets of similar composition but larger—2 by 2 1/2 inches—and pointed at both ends. This owl roosts in low, wet, wooded areas near open country, and its pellets are often found under coniferous trees.

Falcon and hawk pellets have few bones. They usually tear off the flesh of their prey, rather than swallowing it whole. These pellets are composed mainly of fur, feathers and claws. Pellets of the American kestrel, a small, aggressive falcon, can be found by buildings and cliffs near the edges of wooded areas, or near large trees in open areas. These pellets are 1 1/2 inches by 1 inch. The broad-winged hawk leaves larger pellets that are found in the woods.

Another way to locate the roost tree or feeding place of an owl or hawk is to look for the white droppings that cover the branches, trunk and ground below.

In the vicinity of these predators, you can test out what appears to be a paradox. Hawks will not hunt in their own backyard. Small birds and prey seem to be aware of this, and may be found nesting nearby.

Crow pellets consist of seeds, plant stems, tiny pebbles, insect parts and patches of fur, indicating the bird's omnivorous nature. In the winter, they are composed mainly of seeds. The crow's pellets are 1 inch long and usually found in wooded areas.

In more open habitats and along the seashore, the gulls disgorge pellets resembling the crow's in its grab-bag makeup. Gulls eat fish, earthworms, insects and other birds' eggs. It has a huge crop that can hold a whole rat or fish. The gull's pellets are composed of plant matter, fish and animal bones and skull fragments.

Another bird leaves a more gruesome sign behind. The shrike, the only fully predatory songbird in the United States, impales its prey on thorns, sharp sticks or barbed wire. Small prey are eaten at once, head first. Larger prey—birds, rodents, frogs—will be left hung up, for later feeding.

Flight and Migration

Most of us can recognize a flock of birds moving in V formation as Canada geese, but many other birds also can be identified from a distance by their individual or group flight patterns, which are as recognizable as tracks on the ground. These flight patterns are magnified a thousand-fold when the birds migrate.

Goldfinches fly in wavelike patterns. They flap their wings and climb. Then, wings at their sides, they lose a little altitude and flap again. As they fly their hilly path through the sky, they often give a twittering call. Meadow-larks flap their wings several times, glide, then flap their wings again. Chimney swifts have a batlike motion—short, jabbing flaps; they fly high above the ground, their narrow wings beating quickly. Swallows have a similar profile but fly lower to the ground, with less wing flapping.

A few birds can be identified by the sound of their flapping. Mourning doves make a kind of whistling sound as they take off, and the ruffed grouse makes an explosive whir.

A bird's wings are adapted for the particular part of the sky it inhabits. Birds that live close to the ground, like the towhee and pheasant, have short, blunt wings, be-cause they don't fly far but need to be able to take off quickly. Higher up, turkey vultures and eagles have large, wide wings for effortless soaring aloft.

Birds choose their take-off times for their long migra-tions to take advantage of food, winds and cover. Daytime-migrating birds include the stronger-flying smaller birds that catch insects on the wing and those that make short flights, plus most larger birds such as the eastern blue-birds, robins, jays, crows and hawks. Soaring birds, like hawks and herons, migrate during the day to ride the rising currents of air called *thermals*.

Most night-migrating birds are small, weak fliers facing long distances: wrens, woodpeckers and many sparrows. The nighttime flight protects them from the larger birds of prey and allows them to rest and feed during the day.

Large birds that tend to stay hidden, like the wood-cock, also fly at night. Ducks, geese and many shorebirds migrate both day and night. Frequently, birds in migration have been observed awaiting a good tail wind to help carry them north or south. Prior to migration, many birds feed intensely in an area over several days, building up reserves of body fat. Night-migrating birds do quite a bit of chirping to keep the flock together, and possibly to avoid collision.

Birds gain great advantage by migrating in flocks. Flying in a flock protects the birds from attack. Several species of birds—starlings, snow buntings and others—fly in loose formation until a hawk is sighted, then tighten up into a compact flock. By massing, they deter the hawk. A hawk won't dive into a tight flock because it might be injured.

Formation travel makes for more efficient flight. Each bird's path through the air is cleared by the bird in front, increasing the ease with which it can fly—resulting in an up to 71 percent improvement in range, according to some studies. Canada geese fly in a V formation because it enables a strong goose to take the lead and the others to fly in its wake. The lead goose changes frequently, giving the V that shifting quality. The geese have a very identifi-able honking as they pass overhead. Their migration is tied to a chartable change: they follow the 35-degree isotherm (the line of advancing warmer weather) north, allowing them to arrive as the ponds and lakes thaw.

Whistling swans fly in formations similar to the Canada goose, but the swans are larger and the wing beats are noticeably slower. They may, however, fly faster. Their call as they fly is: "Woo-hoo, wow-wow, woo-ho." Snow geese fly in long, wavy lines which are constantly shifting. A flying W is a common formation. They give out a yelp as they go by.

With so many birds flying south, some bird species move north, instead, to the emptier feeding grounds. Cardinals, tufted titmice, Carolina wrens and mocking-birds have all been known to move north in the winter. Robins too sometimes stay up north, making them poor harbingers of spring; since their worm-feeding grounds are frozen, they move into wooded or swampy areas to feed on wild fruits and berries. But most robins do fly south; many will migrate during a cold snap, flying 200 miles a day on their strong wings, returning north once it's warmer.

The birds first to arrive in the north in spring are usually males. They arrive days, sometimes weeks, before the females so they can stake out territory by moving from perch to perch around the periphery, singing all the while. The oldest veterans of this advance group are first to return and reclaim their territory.

Most birds' returns are timed for the most hospitable conditions. The migration of the warbler hits its peak in May, when insects—its primary food—are abundant. Oak trees signal the returning warbler. Oaks wait until spring is firmly entrenched before they put forth their leaves; within days of leafing out, the trees will be filled with the energetic warblers flitting from branch to branch in search of food.

Courtship Flights

Woodcocks begin their "mating dance" just before dark on the first warm evenings of April. This act takes place in a clearing in the woods or brush with a bare spot near the center. The bird lands in this clearing and begins to call ("peent-peent"). Then it flies upward with a twittery sound coming from its wings, climbing in ever-increasing spirals, until it is only a speck in the sky, about 300 feet. There it circles, singing, and then comes tumbling down, leaf-like, making a soft, warbling sound until it is only a few feet from the ground—at which point it rights itself, lands, and starts "peenting" again, preparing to repeat the flight. As the days lengthen, this performance will take place later each evening until June. Try to sit east of the bird to get the best view.

The marsh hawk and the horned lark also have dramatic courtship flights. In March or April the male marsh hawk will begin a ritual by flying upward in very tight circles; on reaching the apex of its flight, it'll drop like a rock to the ground. It seems as if it's about to crash, but at the last moment it opens its wings and rises from the ground. The male will repeat this act until it attracts a mate. Horned larks, too, dive headlong toward the ground, from altitudes of around 800 feet. Up there it has been circling, calling out with a high-pitched, tinkling sound that sounds like small bells from a distance. The horned lark's flight can be observed from February to March.

Bird Baths

Birds bathe in water, dust, sun, smoke and even ants. These are variations of the backyard water bath.

Egrets, herons, grebes and other wading birds and

waterfowl will float on the water, flipping water on their backs with their heads and necks.

Swifts and swallows bathe in flight by splashing across the surface of a lake or pond. After a rain, warblers and other birds will splash about on the leaves of trees and shrubs in what could be called a leaf bath.

Quail, grouse, ring-necked pheasants, house sparrows and others take dust baths, lying down in a sunny, dusty area, and going through the same motions as a water bather.

Sometimes in the summer sun you may see a bird lying on the ground, its back toward the sun, wings and tail feathers spread out, body feathers fluffed; it might be leaning to one side with its bill wide open. It looks like it's dead, but it's merely sun bathing. Birds stay in this position only a few minutes, but the heat helps flush out parasites so they can get at them with their beaks.

Over 200 species of birds are known to put crushed or live ants on their feathers to rid themselves of parasites—so the theory goes, anyway. Robins, blue jays, starlings and cardinals will grasp an ant and rub it over their feathers extremely fast. Some will spread their wings and allow ants to crawl over them. I have most often seen flickers engaged in this activity, and I have seen orioles and mockingbirds do it too. Sometimes you can get a bird to exhibit this behavior by presenting it with a small piece of cloth that has been soaked in vinegar. Why birds "ant" is still something of a mystery. Does the formic acid excreted by ants discourage lice? Does it clean a bird's feathers? Does it sooth the irritated skin that may accompany the growth of new feathers following a molt?

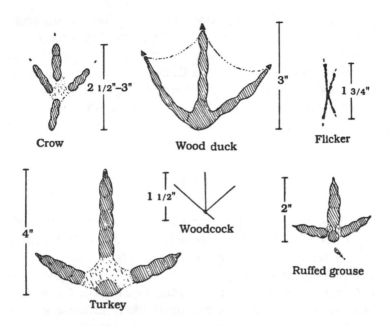

Bird tracks

Bird Tracks

With a few notable exceptions, you cannot track a single species of bird as you can mammals. But the shape and size of the track noted in a particular habitat—shore, meadow or woods—will help you notice what's around.

Birds, of course, walk on two feet. Each foot has four toes; usually, three toes face forward and one angles toward the rear. There are exceptions, though. The yellow-shafted flicker has two toes pointing forward and two pointing to the rear, looking like a splayed H. Other woodpeckers have feet that resemble an X. The inside toes are larger than the outside ones, however.

Birds that spend most of their time in trees will hop along the ground leaving tracks, two by two. Ground-dwelling birds (turkey, quail, pheasant) have a different gait, one more suited to ground travel; they walk along leaving tracks one in front of the other. These ground dwellers usually have much thicker tracks, and the rear toe, if it shows in the track, is usually angled off to one side. There are exceptions, like the junco and robin. These birds live in trees but forage on the ground, and their tracks alternate between hopping and walking.

Water Birds

Ducks, geese, gulls and several other water birds leave webbed prints, extremely toed-in. This webbing shows in a good tracking medium as a faint, concave line, connecting the upper part of the toes like string looping from toe to toe. In gull prints, the fourth rear toe will, at best, be a point. Ducks are most likely to leave a well-defined rear toe print. Tern tracks are a smaller version of gull tracks, about one quarter the size.

The wood duck's track is easily identified. It is webbed and 3 inches long with clear claw marks. The bird uses these claws for climbing.

The great blue heron leaves the largest bird tracks commonly found: they are unwebbed, and 6 1/2 to 8 inches long in a single file. It has an 8-inch to 9-inch stride. The tracks of other herons and bitterns are a similar shape, but considerably smaller.

Dry-land Birds

The pheasant was introduced into the United States from China in the nineteenth century. It lives in open fields, brush areas and crop lands. Its tracks are 2 3/4 to 3 inches long, forming an almost straight line.

The bulges in the toes of a crow are its signature. The

track is 2 3/4 to 3 inches long and its gait is a walk. There is a tendency for the middle toe to drag in the snow. The inner and middle toes are closer together. When it takes flight it often leaves wing marks in snow.

The ruffed grouse is rarely found far from cover. Stands of aspen are favorite winter feeding areas. Grouse grow scales on the fringes of their toes in the winter to help them walk on snow, making their winter tracks much wider than their summer tracks. The tracks are 1 3/4 to 2 1/2 inches in length and the rear toe makes a faint impression.

The wild turkey has segmented calloused pads on its thick toes; this shows up only in excellent tracking medium. The male's tracks are 2 1/2 inches long or longer and the female's are shorter. The hind toe sometimes leaves a print off to one side. The habitat of the turkey is forests, woodland clearings and wooded swamps. It needs open fields for foraging and trees, particularly coniferous ones, for roosting. Turkeys scratch the ground looking for food.

The American woodcock inhabits young woodlands, swamps, stream banks, thickets and fields. Earthworms make up most of its diet. Woodcocks leave long slender tracks: the hind toe is lined up with the outer toe at a 45-degree angle to the bird's path. The one and a quarter-inch-long track looks like a Y with an extra line in the center. They leave a short, zig-zag trail. Look for small holes in the soil where the bird probed for worms with its long beak—a very common sign with these tracks.

4

INSECTS
The Ubiquitous Mysteries

"What sort of insects do you rejoice in where you come from?" the Gnat inquired.
"I don't rejoice *in* insects *at all,"* Alice explained. . . .
—Alice Through the Looking Glass

I am dying by inches from not having anybody to talk to about insects.
—Charles Darwin, age 19,
in a letter to his cousin

I nsects, though we may not want to admit it, have the upper hand, representing 90 percent of animal life on earth. There are an estimated 10 million species of insects, existing in quantity and variety without end. Millions of species are unstudied and uncataloged: 50,000 species of parasitic wasps are known, but there may be 500,000 or more. And that is the news from just one small corner of the insect world.

Above all else insects are adaptable—from the highly
specialized slavery moths that live, prosper and die all
within the fur of the three-toed sloth of South America, to
the cockroach—world traveler, insect-about-town, exem-
plary survivor. (That is, all 3,500 species of cockroach.)

Not surprisingly our tendency is to look around, or
past, insects, as if all these annoyances were just the
Styrofoam® packing of nature—the stuff that falls out of
the box when we go looking for birds or fur-bearing
animals. Yet insects keep everything going, attending to
decay and regeneration. In many habitats, insects are
more important to the environment than four-legged mammals. In a well-known study of 1 acre of English meadow,
there were an estimated 3 1/2 million insects. In one
square inch of soil, there are 6 *miles* of surface area, and
in that teaspoon of soil, 1,356 mites, springtails, milli-
pedes and beetles were found going about their business.

One could go on like this, running up numbers and
superlatives usually reserved for multinational corpora-
tions: millions of species, species of some insect families
outnumbering the stars visible to the naked eye, and so on.
Insects are ubiquitous.

In this chapter we will consider a few of the easily
recognizable ones. All the insects discussed here are
common and make easily identifiable webs, burrows and
nests.

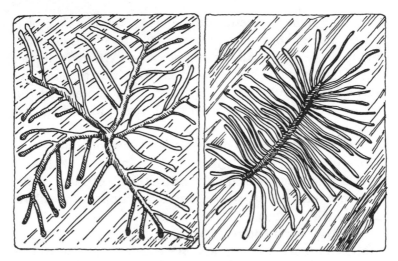

Two types of engraver beetle burrows

Beetles

ENGRAVER (OR BARK) BEETLES

In the past fifty years, the American landscape has been transformed by an insect, one-eighth of an inch long, carrying a fungus. Thousands of towns, cities and college campuses were left barren by the loss of one hundred-year-old elms to Dutch elm disease. The elm bark beetle, which attacked the elms, is one of the many species of engraver bark beetles. Each attacks a different species of tree, engraving a distinct pattern in the layer of wood just below the bark.

You often find these engravings on fallen trees or dead limbs whose bark is missing. By girdling the trunk in great numbers, bark beetles can seriously injure a tree by opening it to infection or fungus.

The burrows of this monogamous species resemble a crew shell with all oars in the water. The burrowing female attracts a male by scent. After mating, the female digs a single, straight burrow about one-eighth of an inch wide, laying single eggs in niches on both sides. When the larvae hatch they begin to burrow and eat their way through the bark perpendicular to the main gallery, the size of the groove increasing in size with the larva, and ending in a round area where it pupates. The American species' main gallery is across the wood grain, with larval burrows going with the grain, so the "engraving" looks like a centipede crawling around the branch's width. It is the opposite with the European beetle, whose engraving appears to follow the branch's length.

Polygamous engraver beetles, such as the Ips bark beetles that attack conifers, leave a different pattern. The male digs a small nuptial chamber under the bark, and with scent, attracts many females. After mating, each female digs her own burrow away from the nuptial chamber, depositing a single egg in the niches on each side of the chamber as she goes. When the larvae hatch, they burrow from the chamber, creating a starfish or snowflake pattern.

The larvae feed, pupate and then bore their way out of the bark, setting out for another tree. These exit holes make it look as if the tree has been hit with birdshot. Scrape off the bark around these holes and you will find the insect burrows.

The ribbed pine borer makes small oval nests under the loose bark of dead pine trees. The nests are made of shreds of wood, one-half of an inch long, and are about 1 inch in diameter. They look like tiny bird nests. There the larva pupates and then eats its way out, leaving behind the nests, which survive for years. They are most common on red pine trees.

WHIRLIGIG BEETLES

Whirligig beetle

The whirligig beetle, true to its name, is continuously whirling and circling, in a merry-go-round of motion. They skate over the surfaces of ponds, each beetle at the center of a ripple of water, always on the hunt for insect larvae or dead insects. Their bodies are a flattened smooth oval, perfectly made for swimming. In some species the lower surface is shaped like a boat keel. The hind legs are paddle-shaped and fringed with hairs. Even though the water may be as filled with these steel-blue beetles as a harbor full of Sunday boaters, the beetles seldom collide. Each beetle is sensitive to the vibrations of other beetles on the water surface, detecting them with a special organ located on the antennae known as *Johnston's Organ*. But if a beetle stops, it is invisible to the other beetles and may be bumped. When alarmed, the beetles move about in interlacing circles so quickly that the eye cannot follow any single one in its mad turnings. The beetles are out in the greatest numbers in spring, when they emerge from their winter holes in the mud.

The whirligig beetle is also a gifted diver. When diving it carries a captured bubble of air under the tips of its wing covers. This shines like a round mirror and can be seen underwater. If you catch a beetle, it sometimes squeaks by rubbing the tips of its abdomen against its wings, emitting a disagreeable milky fluid.

Tent Caterpillars

Three common species of moth larvae construct webbed nests. The eastern tent caterpillar builds its tentlike silk nests during spring. And in autumn the fall webworm builds a nest lined with leaves. The chokecherry tentmaker builds a leaf-filled nest in summer.

The eastern tent caterpillar is found in southeastern Canada and the eastern half of the United States, occasionally in epidemic proportions that defoliate entire areas. The tent caterpillar most often builds its nests in the crotches of trees in the apple, cherry and peach family. When they are spinning, they tend to add more silk to the side of the nest facing the sun, and to orient the tents in the direction of the morning and afternoon sun. They hatch just as the buds of the host tree are opening, and emerge to feed on the newly sprouted leaves beyond the confines of the tent in the early morning, afternoon and around dusk.

The chokecherry tentmaker, or cherry leaf roller, found throughout the United States, builds its nest in early to midsummer in the chokecherry tree. The larvae go to the tip of a branch and pull the leaves in toward the stem, attaching them with their webbing. The tents are long and thin. The caterpillars stay in the nest's center during the day, and feed on the entrapped leaves at night. More leaves are tied into the nest as needed. The chokecherry tentmaker larva makes a cocoon in the web's center and emerges as a pupa that moves outside of the nest and attaches there. In a day or so it emerges as an adult, leaving a pupa shell behind—a clear sign of this species. The tent caterpillar and fall webworm leave the nest to form cocoons, and they pupate in hidden places.

Long after the eastern tent caterpillars have gone on to mothhood, the fall webworm, found in southern Canada and the eastern United States, builds its nest at the tip of branches, enclosing the leaves. It feeds inside its nest, weaving in more leaves as needed, occasionally enveloping several branches of a tree in the web. Nests up to 3 feet long can be found in hickory, elm, pecan and numerous forest and shade trees. In winter the webs look raggy, filled with excrement, debris and the remains of partly eaten leaves.

Galls

At close range nature is deformed; a series of parasitizations and accommodations. There are around 2,000 species of insects that create their housing by secreting chemicals into parts of plants, causing them to grow abnormal structures, called *galls*. Over one half of the families of plants are attacked by gall-making insects. All parts of the plant are vulnerable.

Oaks are infected with more types of galls than any other tree. Oak apple galls, one of the most noticeable types, are caused by members of the wasp family and are found on the leaves: small, green balls about 1 to 2 inches wide. The galls are attached to the leaf's midrib, or its *petiole*, and are filled with a spongy material. At the center the wasp's larvae are enclosed in a hard capsule. These galls turn brown in the fall and can be found hanging on the tree long after the leaves have lost their color. From a distance they look like ornaments. Some oak galls contain such high-quality pigments that the U.S. Treasury, the Bank of England and other national treasuries use them in preparing the inks used to print their currency.

Goldenrod are beset by a number of galls. You cannot walk into a fair-sized field without seeing some. The common elliptical goldenrod gall is caused by a moth larvae. A moth lays eggs on the lower stems and leaves of the goldenrod in the fall. In spring the larvae hatch and

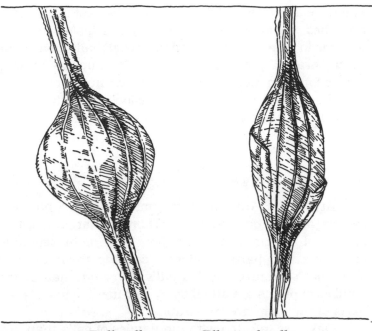

Ball gall   Elliptical gall

crawl toward the newly sprouted goldenrod shoots. It then burrows into the end buds of the plant and digs down into the stem a few inches. There it stops, and the plant forms an elliptical gall around it.

The adult moth emerges from the gall in August or September. No moth larvae will be found in galls on dry goldenrods in autumn. Near the top of the gall will be an exit hole and inside, the reddish-brown skin of the pupa, head up.

If there is a cocoon still inside, this is a sign that the pupating moth was parasitized by one of the several wasps that lay their eggs on the pupa. Many other insects and spiders also find shelter in the abandoned gall.

Goldenrods are also afflicted by a round gall, a ball-shaped swelling on the stem about three-quarters of an inch in diameter. It looks like someone forced a small ball down the stem, midway in the plant. It is caused by the larvae of a small fly. The female lays eggs on the stems in spring, and around June the gall starts to swell. The larvae spend the winter in these galls and emerge in the spring. The larva, however, having secured its home by parasitism, is not safe from becoming a victim itself. It has many parasites, including a small beetle, which eats it and then occupies the gall in winter.

Another gall stunts the growth of the goldenrod, causing leaves to bunch around the gall, making it look like a fat, many-petaled green flower. It is formed by a midge eating into a leaf bud. After the plant has dried, these galls remain, looking like thick feather dusters at the tip of the stalk.

In fact, once you start noticing galls, you'll see them everywhere. Pussy willows in spring may develop what look like 1-inch pine cones, while, in the West, sagebrush develops soft, fleshy balls on the leaves. These are made by a small fly that uses a chemical on the bud to form the gall for larvae.

Praying Mantis

The praying mantis is ferocious in its realm. It will take on and eat almost anything that comes its way—other insects, small frogs, and in one instance, a striped lizard three times its size. The females, as has been well recorded, even devour their mates. Possessing no vicious bite or nasty sting, they are harmless to humans; but if cornered they will put up a fight, jumping out, wings buzzing, and grab on to your finger.

A mantis' eggs are laid in masses of several hundred in a protective brownish froth that dries to a papery consistency. The tan egg cases are usually 3 to 4 feet above

the ground in overgrown, weedy or bushy areas on the
stems of plants. There are three common species of
praying mantis in the United States, each with a different
egg case shape:

somewhat roundish—Chinese mantid;
roundish except for flattened bottom or side—
    European mantid;
flattened oval, attached to support along entire
    length of egg case's flat base—Carolina
    mantid, more common in the South.

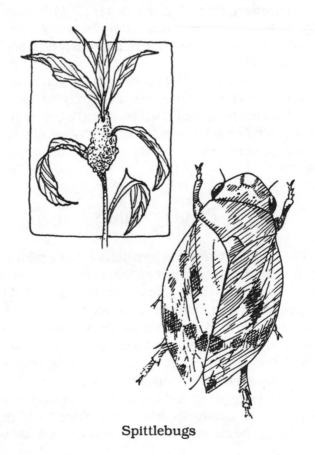

Spittlebugs

Spittlebugs

As a child I used to walk through an abandoned cornfield gone to weed. There were several mysteries about the field, big and little, and one was this: one day it seemed as if some animal had spit on every other weed stalk in the field. Either that, or something was foaming out of the plant. Years later I learned that these frothy bubbles are made by the spittlebug. The larval stage of several different species create these houses of foam as a by-product of feeding on the juices of the host plant. The juice is excreted and frothed up as it passes over little projections on each side of the nymph. This creates a moist environment for the larva and provides some protection from predators. If the nymph is kept from its spittle nest, it will die; its skin is too thin to prevent a loss of moisture.

By pushing aside the spittle, you can see the small, light green or brownish nymph, about one-eighth of an inch long. Sometimes there will be more than one spittlebug in this nest. The spittlebug matures into a drab-colored adult called a *frog hopper*.

Snow Fleas

"The snow flea," observed Thoreau, "seems to be a creature whose summer and prime of life is a thaw in the winter. . . . It is a creature of the thaw. Moist snow is its element." Snow fleas are small creatures, about one-sixteenth of an inch long, which in great numbers look like soot on the snow. A closer examination with a magnifying glass reveals that the soot is hopping about. These snow fleas are actually insects called *springtails* that have climbed up from the soil through the gaps in the snow that form around weed stems and tree trunks. They are able to jump several inches at a time, due to the two appendages at the bottom of the last body segment—their spring tail. These spring-like "legs" are folded against the abdomen and held in place with two clasps. When the clasps release, the legs spring open, launching the insect. They are found in most of the northeastern United States and Canada, north to the Arctic. Some naturalists say snow fleas give off an odor of sliced raw turnips and can be located that way.

Wasps, Hornets and Bees

PAPER WASPS

The paper wasp (*Polistes fuscatus*) is one of the most common wasps, and fortunately one of the least aggressive. Still, it will attack and sting if disturbed. The wasp is three-quarters of an inch long, with a brownish-black body, yellow-orange markings on the abdomen and long legs. Even if you are not in the habit of scrutinizing wasps for their markings, you have certainly seen their nests under the eaves of houses or on the ceilings of attics and barns.

In the spring the queen comes out of her wintering spot and selects a place to build a nest. She forages for wood or paper fibers to build it, scraping and peeling the fibers off dry wood, chewing them up and mixing them with a secretion from her mouth. The nest is attached to a branch or the overhang of a building with a single thread. This single entry can be more easily defended from predators or parasites. In some species the wasp coats the thread with a material that repels ants. The queen also secretes a water-repelling, shiny glaze on the upper side of the nest. The nest looks like an upside-down umbrella with the cells opening on the underside.

There may be anywhere from 10 to 150 cells housing the larvae. (Over 1,000 cells have been reported.) At first the larvae are glued to the nest so they won't fall out.

As many as two hundred adult wasps can be raised in a single nest in one season. Development from egg to adult takes around seven weeks.

In the fall a paper wasp colony will produce male wasps, which are stingless. These males can usually be found feeding on goldenrod pollen. They have a white or yellowish face, while females have dark brown faces. The males are very slow and can be rolled around with a finger when picked up. However, be sure you know what you're doing; there are plenty of yellow and black wasps around that *can* sting.

Sensing danger to their nest, paper wasps assume an alarm posture—wings raised and front legs waving toward the source of danger. Proceed no further. If angry, the wasps will fly directly toward you.

By fall the population has died off. Only the fertilized queen survives the winter by finding a secure spot under some loose bark or in a rotten log.

MUD DAUBERS

Near mud puddles, watch for a wasp on the ground that is tipping forward as if it were about to stand on its head. It will then roll or cut out a mud ball about the size of a pea and carry it off. The black and yellow mud dauber will make about forty of these trips to build one cell in its nest. The nest is a rough-looking clay tube, smooth on the inside, that is usually found on the side of a wall. The mud dauber will leave footprints and tiny holes in the mud where it has been collecting building material.

There are two other species of wasp that build or inhabit mud nests on walls, in attics and other sheltered places. The blue mud dauber makes no nest of its own. It empties out the spiders and eggs from the cells made by the yellow and black mud dauber and puts in its own dead spiders and eggs to feed its larvae. Sometimes this metallic blue-black wasp can be seen carrying water to soften the mud of the nests it is breaking into. They feed heavily on black widow spiders. The pipe organ mud dauber builds nests of mud in long parallel tubes. These tubes may hang on walls singly or in groups, pipe-organ-like, sometimes on top of each other. It, too, is filled with parasitized spiders. The pipe organ wasp is black, sometimes with red markings.

POTTER WASPS

The potter wasp constructs nests that look like small earthenware vases set on twigs. The half-inch-wide vase has a narrow neck and a lip so finely done it looks as if it were thrown on a potter's wheel. The vase nest is built in three to four hours, with a rough outside and smooth interior that is filled with paralyzed cankerworms and other small caterpillars. The wasp, with yellow and black markings, ranges throughout the eastern United States, west to Nebraska and south to Texas.

HORNETS

Hornets and yellow jackets are terms loosely applied to a number of species of the vespid family. In fact, yellow jackets belong to a different subgroup from hornets and build nests underground or in stumps or hollow logs. Hornets usually build large, gray, oval nests up in trees. The hornets construct them by chewing up strips of bark, and mixing it with a glue-like fluid they excrete in their mouths. Look closely at a vacant nest and you can see the different colors of bark used. These are added in curves over the course of a season. The nest will grow until it is about 18 inches long with the entrance off to one side of the bottom.

There seems to be more of these insects around in the

fall because the workers, once tied to foraging in order to feed the larvae, are now free to hunt for themselves, feeding in flowers and trash cans.

BEES

Bees fly a straight line from their hive to the plant they are feeding on and back again. By observing these beelines you can locate the hive and learn which flowers the bees are favoring. Notice how honeybees pick only one species of flower to feed on each day. Bees will move in certain patterns to avoid feeding on the same part of a flower twice. On long-spiked plants, like loosestrife, they will land near the base of the flower and spiral their way up to the top. On large flowers with flat tops, like Queen Anne's lace, or flowers like daisies, bees land at the edge and spiral inward. If you look closely at these flowers, you will find that the smaller individual blossoms are arranged in the same spiraling fashion.

The leaf cutter bee carries a bit of the plant back to the nest. In spring it cuts out small oval pieces of leaf or flower to be used as a small cradle for the young. A food pellet of pollen and nectar is placed in this cradle along with the eggs. The leaf cutter bee's nest is a tunnel in rotten wood or on the ground.

Ant Lion

The ant lion has been setting the same trap for millions of years. In the spring and summer it digs small, conical pits about 1 inch deep and 2 inches in diameter. And there it waits for its prey.

The ant lion is the larval stage of an insect that will end up looking like a damsel fly. The larva—an odd, hump-backed creature with efficient jaws—digs these pits in dry,

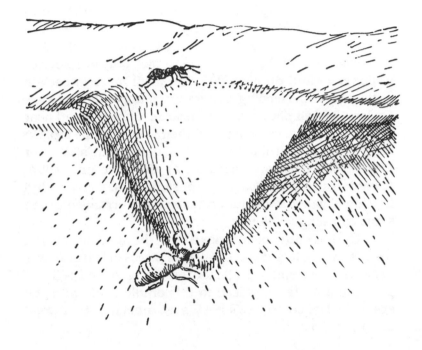

Ant lion trap

fine-grained sandy soil in places somewhat protected from the rain by trees or overhangs. It digs out the pit by backing around in a circle, flicking away dirt from the center with its tail.

Then, on one side of the pit bottom, it settles in to wait. The secret to the success of this trap is that the grains of soil on the sides of the pit are so precariously balanced that only the slightest touch is needed to break them loose and send them tumbling down toward the center of the funnel. An insect happening over the rim is carried to the center by the collapsing wall to the ant lion's waiting pinchers. The ant lion will sometimes flick soil up at the insect to get it to fall farther. Once the ant lion is done with its prey, it tosses the remains out of the pit. After tidying up its trap, it sets to waiting for its next meal.

Sometimes the wait can be quite long. Ant lions are able to endure fasts lasting weeks. They may stay in the larval stage for more than a year if the food that falls into the pit is inadequate.

I've dug out many ant lions to have a look. They remain motionless when disturbed and are covered with a fine layer of dust, making them easy to miss. To see the ant lion in action, take a twig and run it around the side of its pit—it will attack in a flash.

Acorn Weevil

The acorn weevil is rarely seen, staying up in trees, but its handiwork litters the ground. It is a small beetle (1/4 inch long) with a curving beak as long as its body. The antennae are halfway up the beak. This beak has chewing parts that it uses to drill into and eat acorns. The female drills holes into acorns in early summer, lays its eggs and plugs the hole with a fecal pellet, which dries white. After the eggs hatch, the larvae feed on the nut meat and, when mature, bore their way out of the acorn and dig into the ground near the place where the acorn has fallen.

Look through the fallen acorns in the autumn for the ones marked by white dots. If the acorns are soft and there's no exit hole, the larvae are still inside. A hole about the size of a pencil point means they are gone.

Butterflies

MOURNING CLOAKS

The mourning cloak butterfly is the first butterfly I see each spring. But while a welcome sight of spring's renewal, it is also a veteran of the winter, sometimes arriving with torn wings and battered antennae. It is one of the few butterflies in the United States and Canada that stay as adults through the winter. Mourning cloaks, named for the deep purple of their wings, emerge early, well before the trees leaf out, to feed on the rising sap. With wings open, they feed at fresh stumps, broken twigs and branches and tree wounds. They fly by taking several flaps and then gliding. When frightened, they fly to a nearby tree and fold their wings together, hiding themselves by showing only the bark-colored underside of their wings. If the spring turns cool, the butterflies will return to their hibernating places.

The mourning cloak has an odd mating flight. Two will spiral up, about 60 feet in the air and mate. Then one will drop, seeming to faint to the ground. Females lay tiny black eggs on willow, poplar and elm trees. The leaves of these trees are the favorite food of mourning cloak caterpillars.

By late spring there will be few mourning cloaks around. They will have mated, laid eggs and died, leaving another generation to grow through the summer and face the winter.

MONARCHS

From Hudson Bay to the Gulf states, in the fall, all monarch butterflies head south. Annie Dillard, in *Pilgrim at Tinker Creek*, described a monarch in flight as "an

Monarch (left) versus Viceroy (right)

autumn leaf with a will." She watched them overcome hills by flying straight up then gliding down, overcoming houses by flying two stories straight up and cresting the roof with only 2 inches to spare, and so on south to conquer who knew how many mountains, hills, rivers and houses. "Monarches were everywhere," she wrote. "They had but one unwearying thought: South. I watched from my study window: three, four . . . eighteen, nineteen, one every few seconds, and some in tandem. . . .They appeared as Indian horsemen appear in the movies; first dotted, then massed, silent, at the rim of a hill."

All the exertions of the monarch in the fall will bring it south. If they land on a flower, the next one they pick is likely to be south of the first. The return migration in the spring is more gradual. The move northward depends on

the sprouting milkweed. Some of the migrants to the far
northern areas will have been born earlier that same year
on the milkweeds farther to the south.

The black, white and yellow-banded caterpillars of
the monarch eat U-shaped holes on the edge of the
milkweed leaves. If you find these signs, come back and
search the area in about ten to fourteen days and you may
find the chrysalis of these insects, which look like carved
jade trimmed with golden dots at the top. One or two weeks
later an adult monarch emerges.

The adult has a wing span of 3 1/2 to 4 inches and is
brownish-orange, with the wing margins and veins out-
lined in brown or black. The dark margins also have rows
of white or orange dots.

The monarch has a close imitator. The viceroy butterfly has evolved to mimic the monarch's markings. Monarchs, because of their milkweed diet, are inedible to birds.
Milkweed contains poisons similar to digitalis, so birds
spit monarchs out or vomit if they swallow one. The
viceroy, by following under borrowed colors, gains immu-
nity from attack.

There are only two small ways to tell viceroys apart
from monarchs: the hind wings on the viceroy have a black
line that goes somewhat perpendicularly through the
mostly vertical veins. And viceroys glide with their wings
outstretched; monarchs glide with theirs up at an angle.

Another way is the taste test. For many years, before
it was known that monarchs carried poisons, it was
thought that birds avoided them simply because they had
an acrid taste. One expert on monarchs, Dr. F. A. Urquhart,
decided to test this hypothesis: he ate one. The findings
were a bit anticlimactic. Monarchs taste like dried toast.

Moths or Butterflies

There are several ways you can tell moths and butterflies apart:

1. butterflies are mostly diurnal, moths nocturnal;
2. moths at rest usually either stretch out their wings or fold them close to their bodies. Butterflies are likely to keep their wings together straight up over their backs; and
3. moths' antennae are short and feathery, while butterflies have long slender antennae with knobbed ends.

"It is astounding how little the ordinary person notices butterflies," wrote lepidopterist and writer Vladimir Nabokov. And to prove his point he asked people at random if they had seen any butterflies: "'None,' calmly replied that sturdy Swiss hiker with Camus in his rucksack when purposely asked by me for the benefit of my incredulous companion if he [the hiker] had seen any butterflies while descending the trail where, a moment before, you and I had been delighting in swarms of them."

5

PLANTS

Moss on All Sides

We would like to be remembered as a country of trees. We name our streets Oak, Cottonwood, Camellia. Our cities are home to festivals honoring aspen and maple, cherry and dogwood. Trees figure in state flags and city seals. Trees stand tall in childhood memories: tree houses, tree swings. Trees inspire poetry and metaphor. Trees are landmarks in time—our own and our history's.

In our time there are a few big trees left in cities, gone from Dutch elm disease, gone from chestnut blight, gone from parking lot and subdivision development. These were great trees bearing venerated names like Washington and Jefferson, and holding aloft ideas like Liberty.

We mark our history by trees. Those we plant, those we leave standing. And trees make our history and climate and they made our early prosperity.

The trees that stand along roadsides and hedgerows have a history to tell, a story of changes in the land. But the story is told, though more subtly, by other plants as well. Lilacs in the woods by a cellar hole tell of vanished dooryards. Daisies and clover are immigrants along the roadside as new to this continent as we are. Other plants tell of the change from woods to fields and back again, of change in latitude and weather. Plants are the key indicators of the environment. They tell us about the climate, soil and wildlife of an area over the long term. Plants serve as shorthand for the environment; geographers, for example, classify the earth's climatic regions by dominant plant species. And it all follows from there: what types of wildlife, what people eat and wear, and so forth.

The best place to start looking is your own backyard. The variety and number of species on that small patch of earth may be bewildering at first. But once you start looking, you'll develop an eye for plants: which flowers bloom in different seasons and open at what time of day. Get to know the colors and shapes of the predominant plants. Learn to look for these patterns, and as you scan an area those plants will stand out. You'll even be able to spot them from your car. I never miss the bright orange butterfly weeds when they bloom each summer; as I drive by, they catch my eye like a parade of small waving flags.

A careful study of the botanical illustrations in field guides and gardening books will make even more plants seem to step forward from an undistinguished crowd of green. Studying a few plants in these guides is like learning phrases in a foreign language prior to a trip abroad—of the language that flows in around you, there will be islands of the known expressions and greetings.

There are three terms to know when reading anything about plants: *annuals*, *biennials* and *perennials*. Annuals live only for one season. They have rapid growth rates that make them able to quickly occupy newly disturbed areas, such as cleared fields.

Biennials live for two growing seasons. In the first season the plant grows roots and leaves. The leaves are usually roseate and cluster close to the ground. The roots store nutrients for the second season of growth: stems,

flowers, fruits and seeds. The plant dies after the second
growing season. Biennials also grow in disturbed soils,
and can adapt to diverse conditions by delaying their
flowering for an additional season.

A perennial may live from a few years to centuries.
They can produce seeds or spores over their entire life.
They frequently become the dominant species in the area,
outlasting the quick-starting annuals and biennials. In
good seasons they can store food to draw on in lean years.

Immigrants by the Roadside

The landscape we see around us is filled with invad-
ers and vagabonds, plants that are opportunists and
plants that were coaxed and cultivated into becoming a
nuisance. After three hundred years of commerce and
tinkering, America shares much in common with the
Europe settlers left behind. In the Northeast, 18 percent of
the total number of plant species have been introduced
from foreign lands. All these plants represent quite a range
of species, but all are able to thrive on disturbed soils
where the native flora can't compete.

Over half of the plants we call weeds come from Europe.
Most weeds do well in open sunny habitats: the kind of open
land they had been growing in for centuries in Europe. Here,
once the great forest was cleared, these introduced weeds
flourished without much competition. Many of these weeds
we have come to think of as hallmarks of our landscape. It
is a roll-call of the commonplace: oxeye daisy, dandelion,
common chickweed, Queen Anne's lace, chicory, butter and
eggs, common mullein, bladder campion, yarrow, common
mallow, purple loosestrife. Take away these plants, fields of
bright blue chicory flowers or even rolling hills brightly
spotted with dandelions, and our country would seem
foreign to us—as foreign a place as it was to the pioneers.

These plants arrived here in many ways. Some, like Queen Anne's lace and dandelions, were grown as crops during the colonial period in the Northeast. Others were stowaways, coming over in soil used as ballast for empty ships sailing from England to America. The ballast would be dumped in port, thereby introducing new immigrant plants. Others were spread by imported hogs and cattle. One plant, the empress tree, arrived as packing material. Its seed pods were used to pack ceramics and other breakable items.

Quite a few of these plants were spread with the best of intentions. Johnny Appleseed left behind more than orchards in his travels. He propagated certain plants he believed had medicinal powers. One plant he introduced, and for which he will never be forgiven by Ohio farmers, is dogfennel, also known as mayweed. He got the seeds in Pennsylvania and planted them as a remedy for malaria around homesteads. This weed has caused more trouble in the Ohio Valley than the disease ever did.

Multiflora rose, a thick shrub with barbed stems and abundant flowers, has been actively encouraged toward its current nuisance state. It was first introduced from the Orient as rootstock to improve ornamental roses. Later, it was extolled by agricultural agents as an excellent living fence to confine livestock, and then promoted as good food and cover for wildlife (grouse, pheasant, black bears, beavers, cottontails, deer, mice and several songbirds all feed on the multiflora rose). Today the multiflora rose is out of control. In West Virginia, it has taken over more than 1 million acres of land; farmers have abandoned land where the plant has made passage by man or beast impossible. Several states have laws against propagating the plant. And those federal and state agencies that had promoted the plant are now working to eradicate it.

In Alabama, Georgia and Mississippi, another trans-plant from the Orient is out of hand. Kudzu, a high-climbing Japanese vine with graceful purple blossoms is like a green wave covering trees, railroad beds, cars, buildings—anything that sits still long enough. Growing at the horror-movie rate of a foot a day, it fetters stationary railroad cars, and brings down transformers and telephone wires with its weight. Says one Alabama forester, "I get calls from little old ladies who tell me their husbands have died and the kudzu's taking over their houses. They get nightmares about it."

Kudzu was intentionally introduced to the South in the 1920s as a forage crop for pigs, goats and cattle, a situation that has been likened to taking a lion cub home for a pet. Many patches of kudzu have developed root systems that weigh up to 300 pounds, stretching 20 feet underground, making it next to impossible to eradicate.

New plants are still arriving and making inroads. Russian giant hogweed, which can grow to almost 16 feet, is now established in central and western New York state. It was originally introduced as a curiosity and an ornamental plant. The plant can cause severe rashes and blistering and leave scars on some people that last for years. The weed, easily recognizable with its yard-long leaves and umbrella-shaped blooms, grows along stream banks, in roadside ditches and in waste areas where water pools. It produces showy seeds that downy woodpeckers and nuthatches have been seen eating. The giant hogweed, a perennial, is native to the Caucasus Mountains in Russia, and, as they used to say in police shows, may be headed your way.

The spread and profusion of foreign plant life masks the disappearance and extinction of several native species. Applegate's milk vetch, for example, hasn't been seen in Oregon since 1931. The Ocmulgee skullcap was last seen near Macon, Georgia, in 1898. Many native plants are in danger, such as frostweeds, lemon lily, Peebles Navajo cactus and cobra plants. Some plants, in sensitive areas like sand dunes and the alpine zones of mountains, are being trampled into extinction. These are areas where life is slow to take hold, and these plants exist precariously.

Plants as Indicators of the Environment

Early settlers looked for oak, buckeye, maple and walnut trees; signs that the land, once cleared, would be good for grain or hay. In the Great Smokies, blue ash signified good soil for crops. In the West, however, small dwarf oaks indicated hardscrabble—bad farming land. Land speculators sold these "oaklands" to easterners who were taken in, reading the presence of oaks as a good sign.

Today, a heavy growth of certain weeds and wild flowers can serve as tip-offs to soil quality:

- Acid soil: wild strawberries, oxeye daisy, hawkweed.
- Poorly drained soil: mosses, curly dock, Mayapple, Joe-pye weed; also red maple and swamp oak trees.
- Well-drained soil: burdock, chicory, purslane, lamb's quarters.
- Rich subsoil: large Queen Anne's lace. These plants have deep roots.
- Good soil: cockleburr, lamb's quarters, stinging nettle, purslane, giant ragweed. In poorer soil, if they grow at all, these plants are hard to spot.
- Poor soil: Dogfennel, butter and eggs, sheep sorrel.
- Alkaline soil: bladder campion.
- Recently disturbed soil: burdock, ragweed, lamb's quarters, purslane, plantain. Plan-

tain was called "the white man's footsteps," because this introduced weed grew whenever the settlers cleared and worked the soil.
- High water table and underground stream: common rush, horsetail, willows.
- Very wet soil, possibly flooded part of the year: cattails, monkey flower.

Cattails also mark the end reach of salt water in an estuary. Where cattails stand in tall, tight formations, the water is fresh. Marsh elders usually mark the highest water level of the tide marsh washed by salt water. One foot above the mean high water mark there is a band of shrubby bushes where the tide marsh ends, and cedars, junipers, poison ivy and honeysuckle grow. The delineation between salt and fresh water can in turn be used to identify plants. Eelgrass (*Zostera marina*) lives in the saline waters of the tide marsh; while similar-looking water celery (*Vallisneria americana*) grows only in fresh water. The two may be found close together, but they will be in ecologically distinct areas.

Other plants tell of sun and shadow. Trilliums and Mayapples grow best in shade, common mullien and dandelion in direct sun. Sensitive fern, so named because of its acute reaction to the cold, has leaves that turn brown almost as soon as the temperature falls to freezing. It can be an excellent sign of cold pockets that frost over early.

In the Northeast, the settlers' cleared land is now often woods again, the barn and house fallen in, only cellar holes remain. But there are still many other signs of their labors. Lilacs tell of vanished dooryards. Lilacs were planted around early homes and continue to bloom long after wild plants have covered the house's foundation. Clumps of daffodils and day lilies will remain until the forest overwhelms them, and forsythia bushes and Norway spruce will stand as markers of the ghost farm.

Straight lines of Osage orange trees may also remain. These were used as hedge fences by farmers in the East and Midwest.

Moss on All Sides

Moss does tend to grow heavier on the north side of trees, but there are numerous exceptions to this rule. Moss grows only on the north side without exception in one kind of forest: a mature, closely planted primeval stand of woods. In other forests, there are many differing conditions of sunlight and moisture.

Other rules of thumb are more consistent. They concern the two most important shaping forces for plants: the sun from the south and the direction of the prevailing wind. Here are some examples:

- Deciduous trees grow mostly on the south side of hills, but confiers will usually be found on the north slope.
- Trees are often fuller on their south sides.
- Willows, alders and poplars tend to lean toward the south.
- Most bird nests, squirrel nests and even ant hills, in or around trees, are found to the lee of the prevailing wind, often facing south.
- The north sides of most trees in an evenly forested area have thicker bark and wider growth rings.
- The tops of evergreens usually grow away from the direction of the prevailing wind.
- The trunk of the aspen, a greenish yellow bark, tends to be somewhat whiter on its south side. The aspen gets this two-toned appearance because its bark is alive and

photosynthesizing, not a dead layer as it is
on most trees. In winter, with the leaves off
the trees, the tree loses its protection from
the sun on the south side. If the bark became
active in the sun the tree would be killed by
the frost.

Some plants grow so accurately along a north-south
line you can navigate by them. Prickly lettuce grows with
its leaves pointing east and west to gain the maximum
sunlight. It is also known as a compass plant. Seen from
east or west the plant looks quite slim, but when seen from
north or south, it's a wide plant. To figure out which side
is north, judge by the sun's position: prior to noon the
eastern leaves will be on the same side as the sun.

Moss and lichens are more than signposts to be read
in the woods by aspiring Natty Bumppos. Many species of
these plants depend upon wind-carried nutrients, and so
are very sensitive to human-made pollution. In polluted
areas, moss quickly disappears from tree trunks, and
lichens are most noticeably absent. This is one measure-
ment used to gauge air quality.

To understand how sensitive lichens are, take an
example that transverses the extremes of the globe. Lapland,
a region above the Arctic Circle, is 10,000 miles from the
atolls in the Pacific Ocean where the first atomic bombs
were tested. Yet Laplanders have the highest concentration of radiation in their tissues of any people on earth.
Laplanders eat mostly reindeer meat. The reindeer feed
primarily on reindeer moss, lichens which absorb mineral
nutrients directly from the dust in the air. As a result,
lichens have high amounts of radioactive material—and
this only intensifies as you move up the food chain:
reindeer accumulate four times more radiation than the
moss; Lapps have one hundred times more radiation.

Environmental Influences on Plants

Here we hop on a playground carousel: the environment shapes the plants and the plants shape the environment. And so on, in turn. Call it a cycle, a chain or a web, it's only a question of where we get on.

Sunlight is very important in shaping trees. In open fields, trees show their ideal shape, branching out with full crowns. However, they are exposed to winds that can stunt their growth and break branches. In the open, buffeted by winds, trees develop wider bases, where the swaying of the tree causes the greatest strain. In forests, trees stretch to the canopy for light. They have no lower branches and almost perfectly straight trunks. Trees at the edge of open areas, like fields and lakes, lean toward the clearing.

Leaves exposed to direct sun tend to be smaller and thicker than those that are shaded. While leaf shape varies from tree to tree, it also varies from leaf to leaf on a single tree. The leaves on the outermost part of a tree are often smaller and thicker than those on the shadier, inner portions. In general, plants in sunny, dry environments tend to have small, thick leaves to avoid the dehydrating effects of prolonged exposure to direct sunlight and moving air.

Coniferous trees such as the pines, spruce and firs grow in colder areas. Their leaves are needle-shaped and covered with a waxy substance to reduce moisture loss and hold in heat. The interiors of pine needles have been measured to be 10 degrees warmer than the surrounding air. To a tree, winter is like a drought.

In the shade beneath the trees, in eastern woodlands, a plant's life is a competition for light. The amount of light will determine whether a plant has a chance to flower. There are many healthy-looking blueberry plants in my woods that no longer flower and fruit; the canopy has begun to shade them, making the light too diffuse for the plants to reproduce. Flowers, fruits and seeds tend to need intense light; woodland flowers bloom in early spring before their light is cut off.

Many tree trunks dodge and bend, growing around trees that have fallen on them. Trees will swallow old signs, clotheslines, wires, scythes, the bark growing over like a pudding. Years ago, on a trail I knew well, I saw that a tree had been snapped by a hurricane. When I went over to look, I found an iron ring, 5 inches in diameter, inside the trunk. I still have the ring, and I feel that only King Arthur's acquisition of the sword Excalibur may have been more remarkable.

A tree that is bent so its trunk seems to make a right-angle turn has been frequently exposed to winds of 50 miles per hour or more. This happens to trees that grow along stormy coasts and high up on mountains. If this wind were about 10 miles per hour less, the tree would be bent at only about 60 degrees. Trees along a riverside tend to have a many-trunked, broad shape that is rarer among upland trees.

The roots of normally shaped trees usually extend out to the drip line of the branches. As the crown of the trees extends, so do the roots, to catch the rain falling off the leaves.

Trees' Effect on the Environment

Trees strive for light. They grow, leaf out. As the conditions of light are changed, the carousel spins. The trees affect the environment.

Light only seeps into the forest. On a clear day, twilight comes up to sixteen minutes earlier in a deciduous forest than in a clearing and up to twenty minutes earlier in a coniferous forest. On an overcast or rainy day, twilight in a forest can fall forty-five minutes to an hour earlier. Young forests, with a greater crowding of lower branches, let in less light than mature forests. A stand of ten-year-old firs may let in only 10 percent of the light, while a one hundred-year-old stand of the same species will allow 25 percent of the ambient light to reach the ground.

It is usually 5 to 10 degrees cooler in the forest than out in the open. The canopy of the trees absorbs and reflects much of the light. At night, however, it will be warmer in the forest. The day's heat is blocked from rising by the canopy.

To see how forests keep heat in, look at a lone tree still in leaf during a frost in early autumn. There will be a frost-free ring on the ground below the tree's canopy. This effect is multiplied in a stand of trees.

The difference in temperature between a forest and a small clearing can be estimated by comparing the diameter of the clearing with the height of the surrounding trees. When, for example, the clearing is twice as wide as the trees are tall, the temperature in the clearing's center is close to that of open terrain. If the diameter of the clearing is about the same as the height of the trees, the temperature will be equal to that inside the forest. These small clearings are ideal places to camp in the autumn, offering moderate temperatures and a clear view of the night sky.

Just as trees block out light, they do the same with rain. During a light rain, a deciduous forest in full leaf will stop about one quarter of the rain from hitting the ground. In a downpour during a thunderstorm, it will stop only about 2 percent of the water. The intercepted rain, clinging to the leaves, quickly evaporates, keeping the trees' crowns in 100 percent humidity. If the wind gusts and lifts the humid air into the cooler air above the treetops, the moist air will cool down, forming small, ragged clouds or "forest smoke." This lasts for about one hour after the rain has stopped.

Trees also form great windbreaks, as a study of old farms will show. The wind can be eight times as strong out in the open as in the woods. Forests also filter out the dust in the air—around 85 percent of the dust particles in an approaching wind flow are removed before traveling only 100 yards through a forest.

Altitude and Slope

In April, people in mountain settings can see spring moving up the slopes, tree by tree, the hazy green spreading among the trees like a rumor through a crowd. The spread of this delicate springtime hue is clearly visible and easily tracked due to changes in altitude and temperature. For every increase of 300 feet in altitude, the temperature drops 1 degree Fahrenheit, shortening the growing season by five days.

On mountain slopes it is temperature and moisture, not altitude, that determines which plants take hold. The south-facing slopes are hotter and drier than the north slopes, having more freezes and thaws, which cause more soil erosion. Plants that are found at the base of a mountain grow farther up the southern side, as do all other bands of vegetation.

On the south side of the mountain, the conifers and the timberline start higher up than on the north slope. Vegetation on the north slope will tend to be a darker green, because it has more moisture, deeper soil and cooler temperatures. Different species inhabit north and south slopes. For example, hemlock often grows on shady north-facing slopes, while oak prefers the warmer, drier, south-facing exposures.

Plants at higher altitudes have to be able to withstand greater daily extremes in temperatures. The air is thinner and does not hold heat as well. These changes create the horizontal bands seen on mountainsides; each band is a community of plants adapted to the extremes of that altitude. Changes in altitude parallel changes in latitude. For example, some species of plants that are common in more northern states are found only on mountaintops further to the south, and species common in the South are found only in valleys at the northern edge of their range.

Often the same kind of tree will be found at different altitudes on the same mountain, but much altered by wind, temperature and snow. Near the mountain base, conifers have their standard cone shape. Up the slope, nearing the tree line, the trees are rearranged by the wind; they have a much fuller growth on the leeward side of the tree, with few (and sometimes no) branches facing the wind. Even farther up, in the alpine zone, the tree will be misshapen by its efforts to hang on. Known as *Krummholz* (German for "twisted wood"), the trees grow prostrate on the ground, as if ducking out of the wind. Branches on the leeward side of Krummholz trees are sometimes forced into contact with the soil for so long that they actually put down roots.

Spring Blooms

Spring moves north at a saunter, about 13 miles a day. At first, spring presents itself as a series of clues in a snow-covered landscape: the sap starts running in maple trees, the twigs of willows turn yellow, as do the beaks of starlings. In this early pre-spring time (there should be a word for the anticipation of this demi-season) the signs of spring have to be hunted out.

Flowers bloom at about the same time each year. The yellow trout lily in the lowlands is one I always look for first. Keep a diary of the plants you see and you'll soon find the early blooming spots and the progression of flowers. In general, the more botanically primitive flowers, such as trilliums and hepaticas, bloom early in the growing season, while more complex, composite flowers, like goldenrods and asters, bloom late, in September or October. The dandelion is an exception to this rule. In sheltered areas, dandelions and chickweed may bloom throughout the winter.

To find the earliest plant growth in spring, go to sandy woods and look for hills, banks or other areas with a southern exposure. Even though the rest of the woods may be snow covered, plants in these areas will surface and bloom earlier (arbutus, pipsissewa, barberry). If the sun is shining on the slope, and it is sheltered from the wind, you'll find it warm enough to shed your winter coat.

Skunk cabbage

Spring growth starts in the woods and moves out to the open meadows. In the short period of warm weather before the trees leaf out, flowers bloom on the forest floor. There is great color in the woods then: spring beauty, trout lily, wild geranium. Some of these, like the Mayapple and violets, will stay green for the rest of the summer. Others, like Dutchman's breeches, die back after blooming.

Skunk cabbage is another early plant to watch for in marshy areas. In February or March, the pointed tips will push right through the snow. Skunk cabbage actually generates heat to melt the snow. An internal clock converts the starches stored in the taproot into sugars. It can raise the temperature in its immediate area by as much as 20 degrees Fahrenheit, a heat you can feel by putting your fingers nearby.

The dark-colored, horn-shaped structure that first pushes through contains the small stalk covered with flowers. It is protected by hood-shaped leaves that are reddish on the inside. Skunk cabbage gives off a strong odor resembling rotting meat that attracts the recently awakened flies to pollinate it.

Flowers: Color, Fragrance and Survival

The world in bloom appears in different colors to birds, bees and humans. We are most sensitive to greens and greenish-yellows, and reserve green to represent spring, fertility and peace. Birds are more sensitive to yellows, oranges and reds. They can see differences in reds lost to us, but they cannot match us in discriminating between shades of blue. A flower that relies on birds such as the hummingbird for pollination is usually yellow, orange or red—colors that are about one-third more intense to a hummingbird.

Insects cannot see reds very well, but they can see the many blue and yellow flowers as well as white (which reflects all colors). They also see some light from the ultraviolet spectrum.

Flowers pollinated by insects have large blossoms or groups of many smaller blossoms. These flowers are often marked with lines, dots and shaded areas that are actually "nectar markers," which guide an insect toward the nectar and the pollen. Some of these nectar markers are visible only in ultraviolet light.

Bees see ultraviolet light, but not the color red; to them, red appears as black. "Bee flowers" often have showy blue or yellow petals—never red. They also have nectar guides, which run from the outer edges of the petals down the tube of the flower. Some of these flowers have semi-closed flower throats to keep out weaker insects.

The right insect must be attracted to the right flower. Red clover, for example, can be polli-nated only by bumble-bees. Other insects, like butterflies, do drink its nectar, but do not carry the pollen to the next clo-ver.

Years ago, Austra-lian farmers introduced red clover to their conti-nent as fodder for sheep and cattle. The first year

Evening primrose

they had an abundant crop, but the next year there was not a single plant. The clover did not reproduce because there was no native insect able to pollinate it. The following year the bumblebee was imported, and the clover took.

Flowers pollinated by diurnal moths or butterflies are similar in many ways to those pollinated by bees. Some butterflies, however, can see the color red, and will visit red-orange flowers like butterfly weed.

Nocturnal moths have a good sense of smell. Night-blooming flowers that are pollinated by moths are usually white, pale yellow or pink, with a sweet, heavy fragrance, such as the evening primrose. These flowers have deep tubes to allow only moths to get the nectar. Notice how moths hover over flowers rather than landing on them as do butterflies.

During the day, evening primrose is not much to look at, with its wilting, faded flowers, stumpy capsules and narrow leaves. But at twilight, the buds open, and yellow, lemon-scented flowers appear, glowing with that soft indistinctness of twilight. Evening primrose depends on night-flying moths, and its nectar is too deep for all but moth tongues.

Honeysuckle and swamp azalea are also more fragrant at night, so as to attract moths. They, too, have long flowers that protect their nectar from bees and flies. The night-flowering catch-fly opens its white and pink blossoms at dusk. The stems have sticky hairs to discourage crawling insects. This plant was once cultivated.

Beetles were probably the earliest insect pollinators. Flowers pollinated by beetles are usually large (or grouped into large inflorescences), dull-white or greenish in color and shaped like open bowls. Beetles have a better sense of smell than vision, and are attracted to fruity, spicy fermented odors as well as carrion and manure smells. Dogwoods, magnolia and Queen Anne's lace are beetle pollinated.

Some flowers stink, though they may look pretty enough, even inviting. I once stuck my nose into a wake-robin—a beautiful red flower of spring—and was astounded to learn that it smells like rotting flesh (the better to attract flies).

To wake-robin you can add the carrion flower, which smells like decaying meat, and skunk cabbage and the stinkhorn mushroom. Taken together, this is a bouquet not likely to be found at the local florist, but it is a very attractive scent for flies, who are their main pollinators.

Wind-pollinated flowers are dull-colored and relatively odorless. Their petals are small and absent and their stamens are exposed to the wind. They produce more pollen than insect-pollinated plants, since the odds of each pollen grain landing on a flower of its own species are low.

Fall Colors

The northern limit of broadleaf trees is approximately 150 miles north of Montreal. Sometime in August the leaves on these trees start changing and autumn has begun. Fall colors will move south, in the United States, about 33 miles a day. As autumn arrives there is a set sequence among the trees: The sumacs turn first, deep red and purple. Then the reds and oranges of the maples, and the yellows of birches and hickories, followed by the reds and browns of oaks, and ending with the burnt orange and yellows of the beeches.

In the fall, a corky layer at the base of the leaf seals off water and food from the leaf, sending it to its beautiful death. The pigments that color the fall foliage are present in the leaf throughout spring and summer, but the green pigment, chlorophyll, overshadows them. During the growing season, chlorophyll is broken down and replaced by the plant. As the days get shorter, more chlorophyll is broken down than is replaced. When the chlorophyll is gone, other pigments in the leaf, such as carotenoids, which are yellow, dominate, producing a different color in each tree species.

Cold nights (not freezing) and warm, Indian summer days produce the most dramatic fall colors. Below freezing weather will turn the leaves a withered brown, and a hard rain will knock the leaves off.

Two broadleaf trees, beeches and oaks, hold on to their dry brown leaves until the new ones of spring push them off. They are easy to identify in winter. Beech leaves are usually a lighter tan than the dark brown oak leaves, and the bark of beeches is smooth and gray. Oaks have a rougher, brown bark.

The pioneers in the East used the dry beech leaves to stuff mattresses. They found the leaves springier, softer and longer-lasting than straw.

The last flowers of the year are found on witch hazel. These yellow flowers have long, narrow, crumpled petals. The flower blooms just as the plant is losing its leaves, producing a woody seed capsule that it will later launch up to 20 feet away.

The Age of Trees

A tree is history—a history of rainy springs, flash fires and cleared land. Each year, trees add a ring of growth, a new layer of wood just below the bark. Each annual ring is made up of two segments. The light portion of the ring is laid down during the rapid growth of spring and early summer; the darker bands are formed at season's end.

The annual rings on a freshly felled tree or its stump have much to tell about the history of the tree and its sites. (The higher up a tree is cut, the more likely some early rings will be missing.) Wide, even rings show good conditions—

Budscars (left) and annual rings (right)

plentiful sun and rain—and fast growth. Narrows rings indicate poorer growing seasons, competition from other trees and pests. Signs of fire will show as a burn mark on a tree ring (thus dating the fire); the side that the fire mark is on is where the wind most likely blew from that day. The tree's branches will show as knots. These are the bases of branches that the tree, growing outward, has covered over. There are more knots at the tree's center, formed when the tree was smaller and had more branches close to the ground. Groups of narrow rings followed by wider rings indicate a drought cycle in the area. This can be checked against the weather records and used for some cracker-barrel forecasting.

However, a tree may have grown slowly even in a good season—it may have been shaded out by competing trees. By comparing the rings of several trees you can tell the cause. If the pattern is regular and common to trees in the area, it is possibly due to weather conditions. If one tree does not correspond to the pattern, competition most likely limited its ring size.

Analyzing tree rings in this manner can show in broad outline when that plot of land was last cleared (or burned) and how it grew back. At the time of clearing, a tree may show good growth, followed by smaller and smaller rings. Early on, the tree had a jump on all others, but as the field grew back, it was running a poor second to the newer tree. That second tree will show narrow rings at the center and then a period of wider rings.

Sometimes trees can show two rings for a single year's growth. An unseasonably cold snap can abruptly end the growing season. Once it warms up, growth resumes. An intermission in growth may also occur if the tree is defoliated by insects. All growth will stop until the tree leafs out again.

The term *growth rings* may be deceptive. They are not always that uniform. A single ring may be wider on one side than another from certain stresses, like a tree falling on it or strong winds stunting the growth on the windward side. The tree will attempt to straighten itself, either by pushing or pulling. In deciduous trees, the thin side of the ring is caused by the tree contracting the new cells on the outside of the bend, pulling the tree straight. Evergreens expand on the underside of the bend—pushing the bent tree up. This difference in strategy is also imprinted in the branches. The rings on most hardwood branches are thicker on the top side, and most pine branches are thicker on the lower side.

A rough way to gauge the age of a tree is to measure its girth 5 feet up from the ground (standard height). The number of inches in girth roughly equals the tree's age.

To date a pine tree is even simpler. Pine trees grow a new whorl of branches each year except in the first three years of life. The most recent years' growth is at the top. The distance between one level of branches and the next

represents one year's growth, particularly the first six
weeks of spring, when it grows the most. To gauge how tall
the pines in the forest were, say, ten years ago, look up to
the top of the tree and down ten whorls.

Branches, Bud Scars

A growing season can also be read in a tree's branches.
Buds do not burst on the scene in spring. Rather, they are
formed the previous summer, lie dormant through winter
and, on those species with terminal buds, are protected by
scales that completely encircle the bud. These scales fall
off in the spring, leaving a scar encircling the twig. If you
measure the distance between two of these bud scars, you'll
know how much the plant grew that year. Count back four
scars and you'll know how long the branch was four years
ago. Horse chestnut trees are good ones to start on; the bud
scars are very clear. In autumn, winter or early spring, look
back from the terminal bud to the first set of bud scars—that
is the growth of last summer. If you are observing this during
the summer, the distance from the last bud represents the
growth of the present season. The scars can be used to
compare growth on different branches of the same tree or
shrub, and among different trees. Bud scars are visible for
several years until covered over by bark.

A number of trees (such as willows and birches) and
shrubs have false terminal buds. These plants will not
have the encircling bud scars and cannot be dated with
this method.

Succession

Three hundred years, in nature, is a wink of time.
Throughout most of the Northeast, this is what you would
see in that wink:

The tall forests standing silent. Then cleared—trees felled, land burned over, a stumpy, stubbly field. The land fenced, farmed; houses, barns; seasons of plenty and seasons of drought. Then, abandonment. Migration, 150 years after clearing. Fields gone to weed, chickweed first, then goldenrod. A barn sags in summer as if it still carried winter's snow. Ten, fifteen or twenty years on, fields, once laboriously cleared, have gone to sumac, blackberries, red cedar. A house now falls into its cellar hole, the end walls coming together like shoulders in a shrug. Pine trees now coming up in the fields and growing in thick, choking out the thickets, growing right in a cellar hole. The chimney has fallen into a pile of stones. Lilacs still mark the long-gone gate. Under the pines, small oaks coming on. Now the land has almost come full circle. Oak trees grow up, take hold. The forest has reclaimed the land.

Plants are constantly replacing each other. The very plants growing in an area may change the environment enough for other species to move in; they can alter themselves out of a home. This is called *succession*. And it will continue—one set of flora succeeding another—until it reaches a point of relative stability, called the *climax stage*. At this stage, the plants are well adapted to climatic conditions, and their own seedlings will fill in any openings. It can take well over a century to reach this stage.

There are two types of succession. *Primary succession* starts in environments previously uninhabited by plants, often with lichen and moss beginning the entire soil-building process from bare rock. *Secondary succession* is the return of plants to an area disturbed by farming, fire or storm. The soil is intact and the higher plants begin the march toward climax vegetation. If there has been much soil erosion, the secondary succession will be similar to the primary one, with plants that rebuild soil moving in first.

Primary Succession: Cliffs, Ponds

A good example of primary succession is found at the edge of a rocky cliff. The bare rock at the edge is the uncolonized area, but just back from it there will be spots of lichen, the "hardiest of pioneers," enduring the extremes of hot and cold (the rock heats up rapidly in the day and cools at night) and of flood and drought (rainwater pools on the cliff, but quickly evaporates). Often, behind the lichen will be a fringe of moss, usually quite noticeable, growing on a thin toupee of soil (which has probably been colonized earlier by lichen). And behind the moss (and mixed in a bit) will be some grasses able to thrive in the thin soil. The soil is deeper behind this, and the established plants of the area are present.

Another type of primary succession can be seen around the edges of ponds and lakes. There the plants, in a sense, walk toward the center of the pond, filling it in.

The lake or pond slowly fills with silt and other organic debris, and the plants invade from the banks toward the center. Once submerged plants take root in the mud along the banks, the build-up of silt is much quicker. As the pond fills up, arrowheads, pickerelweed, reeds and cattails take root in the silty bottom of the shallower waters. The filling continues to accelerate until true terrestrial plants are now on what was, years ago, the shallow reaches of the water. The lake is shrinking, becoming a bog, and finally dry land. It will take thousands of years to go from lake to forest.

Secondary Succession: Old Fields

In an old field that is left untilled, the return of the forest is preceded by a sequence of weeds, thickets and shrubs.

At first the annuals will thrive on the exposed soil. Many of these pioneer plants are ones we refer to as weeds, such as chickweed, ragweed and crabgrass. There is a reserve of dormant seeds from annuals in the soil; some can lie latent for one hundred years. Perennials cannot lie dormant; they must reach suitable soil or perish. Most perennials in the early stages of succession are blown in on the wind.

In the second year, the biennials begin to come into their own, plants like Queen Anne's lace, with its umbrella-like cluster of tiny white flowers, and common mulliens, a tall stalk of yellow blooms. This is the second year for these plants. The year before, they were just a small patch of green leaves on the ground, storing up energy for the next year's growth. These plants will die at the end of the second year, completing their cycle.

By the third year, perennials adapted to soil that is recently, but not newly, disturbed, will appear: goldenrod, yarrow, butterfly weed and Canada thistle. In fact, by the third to fifth season, the field may be dominated by perennials such as goldenrod and asters. There are over one hundred species of goldenrod in the United States (making them hard to tell apart), and the appearance of goldenrod is a clear sign that a field has lain fallow for at least three years.

Among the perennials, in the third or fourth year after abandonment, there are some plants with woody stems. By the fifth or sixth year these plants will be quite conspicuous, making the field a thickety tangle: sumac, blackberries, multiflora rose, honeysuckle. Among this thicket, shrubs and seedling trees begin to show up.

After about a decade, coniferous pioneer trees, like red cedar, start to crowd out the woody shrubs. The trees' shade will kill off the early weeds and shrubs. As the coniferous trees grow closer and closer, soon their own seedlings are shaded out and are blocked from taking root by a blanket of needles. This stage may last twenty years to a half century or longer.

Next come the wind-borne seeds of deciduous trees such as the red maple and the tulip tree. These seeds sprout in the shade, and in time become an understory in the piney woods. As the pines die off with none to replace them, these trees move into their place.

Finally, the acorns and nuts planted by squirrels and blue jays sprout and replace these trees just by outliving them.

In an abandoned field, surrounded by woods, the red maples and black birch should all be a uniform size, since their seeds are spread by the wind, covering the field in one generation. Oaks, on the other hand, have heavy seeds that fall near the tree and rely primarily on squirrels to carry them. The oaks will be older at the field's edge and younger near the center.

As the forest comes to be dominated by oaks and hickories, it has reached an equilibrium, the climax stage, and will continue this way unless altered by catastrophe: fire, bulldozer or some change in climate. It has been fifty to one hundred years since the field was abandoned, a wink of time.

Early and Late Succession

In an abandoned field, the race between plants to take hold can be likened to the fable of the tortoise and the hare. The early plants in succession are the hare in the race: they grow faster than the later trees and shrubs, recover quickly from damage, reproduce at an early age, have lighter seeds that take to the wind and are simpler and shorter lived. The later trees in succession are the tortoise: slow-growing, with deeper roots and heavier seeds that are spread by birds and other animals. And, as in the fable, it's these trees, slow at the starting line, that dominate and win. The shift from annuals to biennials and perennials is a shift from hares to tortoises—from the quick-growing mass of goldenrod to the less numerous, upward-inching oaks.

In general, succession moves from simpler plants to more complex, from a variety of species to a few. The field can also be pictured as growing more shady. Early on the plants require a flood of sunlight. Later plants often require some shade as seedlings. The early plants also shade out their offspring, which can't grow in the shadow of their parents, and so give way to the next generation in the field, the shade-tolerant plants.

Seedlings and Light

In woodlands, there are four distinct layers of life: grasses, mosses and ferns on the forest floor; a layer of shade-tolerant shrubs; an understory of young, shade-tolerant trees; and the canopy of the mature trees.

Trees that demand strong light to take hold have open crowns and trunks clear of all but the topmost branches. Trees that do well in shade have dense crowns and leafy branches close to the ground. Some of these trees, like beech and hemlock, can bide their time through decades of slow growth until there is an opening in the canopy.

The seedlings of each tree species have different light demands:

- Grows well in shade: sugar maple, beech, fir, white cedar.
- Tolerates shade: elm, white oak, red oak, black oak, ash, white pine.
- Light-demanding: silver maple, birch, poplar, willow, larch.

Animals and Succession

On a clear plot of land growing back to forest, it is as if the earth were made new again. Each plant arrives in its turn, and following them, the animals arrive, not in a burst from the ark but also taking their turns.

Each stage of the succession of a field will be inhabitated by different animals. Look back at the habitats of the tracking chapter and it can be read as a roster of the animals that arrived during secondary succession.

The first insects on the scene are much like the plants: opportunists, highly mobile and able to rapidly invade a changed area, with a diet not tied to any single plant. They have short-lived—but large—generations (two or more a year) and since they overwinter as adults, they are ready at the starting line in the spring. The later insects will be larger, and have lives bound up with specific plants.

During the early years of succession, the field will be home to birds that nest on or near the ground, such as field sparrows and yellow-throated warblers. After ten to twenty years, as the field grows into shrubbery and small trees, look for brown thrashers and gray catbirds. As the tree trunks fill out, chickadees and woodpeckers will arrive.

The greatest number of bird species will be found when the field has not been tilled for ten to twenty years, and is changing from weeds to woody thickets and shrubs. Many of the birds that arrived with the pioneer plants are still present, despite the thickets that have attracted new birds. Older fields that are mostly thickets and young woodlands will support a greater number of birds, but with less diversity of species.

6

WEATHER

The Ocean in the Sky

There are places in the country where the land opens up and the continental sweep of the weather is revealed. Up in the topmost county of Maine—Aroostook—where it is all potatoes and lumber, they call the sky "The Aroostook Ocean." There is an ocean passing over our heads daily. In the Midwest, where the land itself is an old ocean bottom, the drama of the sky takes the place of mountains in another topology. One unaccustomed to the Midwest might at first see only the monotony of the land. An easterner, settled in Chicago for two years, was talking about the flat-out sixteen-hour return drive she faced, but then her expression quickened: "One thing about the Midwest: the sky—it's so big—you can see entire storms forming over Lake Michigan."

The scale of the weather is epic—vast enough so that it takes a satellite to order it into patterns of swirl and blue. But in each valley the weather is different. There are signs of approaching rain known to Aroostook farmers and different signs known to farmers in Ada, Ohio. On the East Coast, the seagulls flying overhead and the smell of sea air

35 miles inland is a sign of coming rain.

The best place to predict weather is your own locality. The TV weather is given for wide areas, but with local knowledge you can out-predict the TV meteorologist, or at least refine the predictions for your immediate area. This chapter is about learning to predict the weather. It's not about charts and instruments, but about becoming clued in to the signs around: the changes in wind direction and cloud formation, the way smoke rises from a chimney, the activity of animals and the changes in plants. Using combinations of these signs makes for an accurate prediction. It is asking to be disappointed if you depend on only one sign when predicting the weather. Always look for another sign to confirm the first.

Clouds

Clouds are weather waiting to happen. The myriad of water droplets or ice crystals that make up a cloud ride the ascending air currents like a sailplane. It takes air movement of only one-tenth of a mile an hour to support and move a cloud. As the thermal uplifting of the air ceases, the droplets fall and evaporate in the warmer air at lower altitudes.

The altitude of clouds, and their numbers, provide an introduction to the weather in your area. Read broadly it follows this way:

Bad weather is on the way with an increase in cloud cover, lowering clouds and darker clouds. Rain or snow are likely when these low clouds move in after middle or high clouds. But if clouds stay high, moving with the prevailing winds, it will be fair. When the dark clouds become lighter and the low clouds change to higher types of clouds, the weather is clearing.

Clouds are classified by their altitude—high, middle, low—and by their shapes. There are two basic shapes of

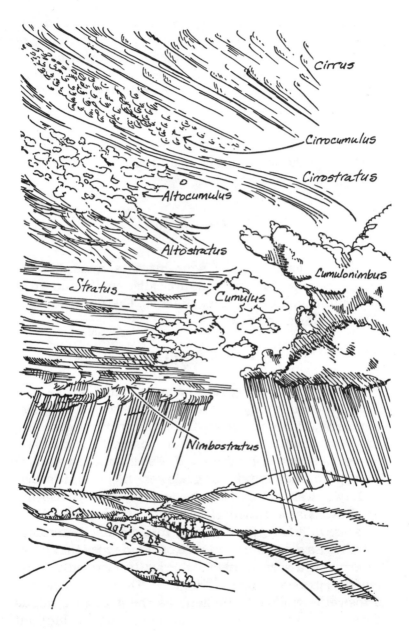

Cloud types

clouds that appear at all altitudes: *cumuliform* and *stratiform*. Cumuliform (meaning "heaped up") look lumpy or billowy, much like mashed potatoes. Stratiform (meaning "spread out") are long, level clouds looking like white sheets. Stratiform are formed when entire layers of air cool until condensation has taken place.

The cloud types discussed in this chapter are only those with some value in predicting the weather. Clouds can indicate the arrival of fronts, and these fronts bring the changes in the weather.

Fronts

Air moves in large cells, or currents, much like the ocean. The edges of these cells are called *fronts*, and when two fronts collide the weather changes. There are two types of fronts: warm and cold.

WARM FRONTS

Warm fronts bring rain or snow. They can be predicted between twenty-four and seventy-two hours before they arrive. Cirrus clouds are the first sign of an approaching warm front. Cirrus are thin, wispy, high clouds—horses' tails tossed by the wind. Essentially, as a warm front approaches, the clouds get lower, thicker and darker. As the warm air arrives it climbs over the cold air mass (hot air always rises), causing the warm air to cool and the moisture in it to condense—first into clouds, then rain.

There's a definite sequence of cloud types that tell of the arrival of a warm front of stable air. It starts with a clear day, the cirrus high up (25,000 feet). Then a thin sheet of cirrostratus gradually thickens as the gathering clouds lower to become blue-gray veils of altostratus, washing out the sun. Six to twelve hours later come the rain clouds—

nimbostratus and, the thick cloud cover, stratus—of a dreary day. Stratus clouds resemble a layer of fog, and are quite low—anywhere from slightly above the ground to 6,500 feet. They may bring rain, but it will never be more than a lingering drizzle.

When the air of a warm front is unstable, there will be thunderstorms interspersed with the drizzle. (Thunderheads—cumulonimbus—will be present above the thick layer of nimbostratus rain clouds.) As the front passes overhead the weather gets warmer, more humid and overcast. Then, gradually, the sky clears and the temperature rises.

In cities known for their overcast skies, stratus clouds will settle in for what seems like weeks on end, a low gray ceiling, until you are walking a bit hunched over. When the sky opens blue—an unbelievable relief—it feels as if you can stand tall again.

On most overcast days you can still find the sun at noontime. The sun is 4,000 miles closer to the earth at midday and it often breaks through the cloud cover as a pale disk.

On clear days man-made clouds can be visible far overhead. High-flying aircraft leave condensation trails (*contrails*) as water droplets in the warm exhaust freeze into ice crystals. These contrails can be read for changes in the weather. A contrail that quickly dissipates means that the air is dry: fair weather ahead. Long-lasting contrails mean the air is moist. This can be a sign of bad weather moving in, particularly if cirrus clouds are present.

Let's run that sequence of approaching rain from a warm front once more. Imagine a time-lapse photo of the approaching storm, twenty-four hours diminished to a few minutes. You set out in the morning. The sky is clear, a few cirrus clouds: picnic weather. The clouds gather into bands, a little thicker now: cirrostratus. They lower some, and are grayer; altostratus have blown in. It's a little cooler now, the sun is only a milky presence. Time to end the picnic, go home, shut the windows. A few hours go by. Dark, low stratus or nimbostratus clouds arrive, and it rains.

COLD FRONTS

Cold fronts bring the most violent storms, give the shortest warning of their approach, and don't linger very long. When the cold air of the front overtakes and rams its way under the warmer air, it makes for some very lively weather.

The first signs of an approaching cold front are the altocumulus clouds, which look like a fleet of white puffs sailing in groups or lines across an otherwise clear sky. These altocumulus clouds build up into cumulonimbus—the clouds that pile up before an advancing front.

Thunderstorms, hail storms and other violent weather can be expected from a cold front. The winds will shift as the front comes in, swinging from the west to the southwest and then to the south, counterclockwise. The air will be humid with expectation. As the storm itself arrives, the wind will veer and come from the north or east. As the front passes, the wind shifts to the west or northwest, the barometer climbs and the air is cooler and drier.

Altocumulus clouds form at the middle altitudes (10,000 to 20,000 feet) and are associated with cold fronts. These are fair-weather clouds, white or gray, and are usually arranged in groups or lines, frequently described as "sheep backs." They don't produce rain, but when these clouds are followed by low altitude clouds, wet weather is at hand.

Not all cold fronts produce dramatic cumulonimbus clouds and the accompanying thunderstorms. If the cold front is slow moving and the warm air is stable, there will be merely a layer of stratus clouds and some rain.

Storm Warnings

Cumulus are brilliant white cauliflower clouds. These are the ideal clouds we remember from childhood days of lying back and watching the summer skies. They are formed by warm air rising up from land that has been heated by the sun. When there are only a few white cumulus clouds in the sky, it is a sign of clear, bright weather. As they begin to build taller and develop flat gray bottoms, look for showers and gusty winds. These can build up farther into thunderheads (cumulonimbus). Thunderheads may be several miles across and up to 10 miles high, with an anvil-shaped head. The height of cumulus clouds indicate the force of the impending storm. At times a continuous line of thunderclouds may build up along the forward line of a front, forming a "squall line."

A day may start clear and build toward thunderstorms. If by 10:00 A.M. or 11:00 A.M. there is little wind and the puffy cumulus clouds are growing in size and weight, there is a good chance of a storm by late afternoon or evening.

When clouds at different altitudes are moving in different directions, it is a sign that a strong storm is headed your way. If you stand with your back to the lower wind (sometimes the lower clouds move with this wind) and the upper clouds are coming from the left, the weather will usually get worse. If the upper wind moves in from the right, the weather should improve.

There is indeed, as the saying goes, a calm before the storm. This will last twenty to thirty minutes and it is a time of great clarity: the smells are stronger, you can see farther and sounds carry more distinctly.

The low pressure that precedes the storm allows odors to rise and diffuse; flowers, swamps and barnyards all smell stronger. Most of the dust in the atmosphere clears in a low-pressure system and distant objects appear closer and clearer. Pick a distant object and observe it daily for clarity and detail. When it looks far away and hazy, expect fair weather. When it looks clear and close up, there is a storm approaching—"The clearer the sight, the closer the rain."

Sounds carry longer distances before and during rainstorms. Where I used to live, you could hear the church bells in the next town only before a rain. Those bells proved to be a reliable sign of rain approaching. Listen for the sounds in your area that you can hear only before and during rainstorms.

Smoke from a campfire or chimney that is curling downward or wafting horizontal is a sign of rain. The smoke stays low due to increased humidity and the downward flow of air in a low-pressure system. Smoke rising straight up and away is a sign of fair weather. In the hearth, a hardwood fire will make little explosions and poppings if rain is due. Fires are harder to kindle, but hotter and brighter right before a storm.

The rise in humidity before a storm causes other changes: wooden furniture that has been treated with oil, feels damp. Brick walls, and many rocks, sweat as the air becomes saturated.

The last moments before a summer storm breaks are my favorite. The pressure builds up, squashing the heat of the day down upon you, then the winds pick up, cool winds, bringing the smell of rain. Then there is a pattering sound, drops of rain leaving little craters in the dust, small puffs of dust rising, and then the winds come up stronger, swaying the tops of trees. The skies darken, the temperature drops perhaps as much as 10 degrees, and the rain falls hard. It is heaviest for the first two or three minutes after it starts. The larger the raindrops, the more severe the storm. After half an hour, the storm has moved through and the air is cooler, much cooler.

The Wind

The wind brings the weather. Each region's weather patterns differ. In the East, a west wind traveling over dry land brings clear weather. But west of the Cascades, a wind from the same direction foretells rain, since it has come in over the Pacific.

In short, east of the Rockies, fair weather comes from the north, northwest, west and southwest. Wet weather arrives on winds from the northeast, east, south and southeast. (Winds are named for the direction they blow from. If you turn north, and the wind is blowing directly in your face, it is a north wind.)

Here, in more detail, is what to expect from the wind's direction:

- North: in summer, cool; in winter, cold.
- Northeast: in summer, cool with rain; in winter, snow.
- East: rain (east of the Rockies).
- Southeast: heavy rain.
- South: warm with showers.
- Southwest: fair and warm.
- West: fair (except Florida and the Pacific Coast).
- Northwest: fair and cool.

On the Atlantic side of the United States, wind from any eastern orientation means rain or snow is imminent. A southeast wind means rain soon, a northeast wind brings storms. If the northeast wind holds after the storm, then the cold will be damp and bitter.

A shift in the wind will bring a change in the weather. A clockwise wind shift (veering) indicates improving weather. During rain, it presages clearing. Clockwise wind shifts (south to west, for example) are part of a high-pressure cell. Backing winds, shifting in a counterclockwise direction, indicate low pressure and foul weather. A backing wind (west to south) in fair weather is a sign that bad weather is on the way.

Near the sea or large lakes, the wind changes direction at different times of the day. On a summer day, with the land heating up faster than the ocean, the hot land air rises, and the cool ocean air breezes in. At night, the land cools quicker, and there is an equally welcome offshore breeze.

In general, winds subside in the evening, as the temperature falls. If the wind does blow all night, you probably are in for rain.

To keep an eye on the shifting winds in your region, find a flag pole in an open area. Use a compass to learn the directions around the pole. Then just watch the flag and you'll know which way the wind is blowing. Another way to find the wind direction is to wet one of your fingers and hold it aloft. One side will feel noticeably cooler. That is the direction the wind is blowing from.

Wind Speed

Wind speed can be determined by watching swaying tree tops and branches, smoke from chimneys and the surfaces of lakes and ponds. These signs are fairly accurate and can be read as follows:

- Less than 1 MPH: Mirror-still water surfaces. Smoke rises straight up from campfires and chimneys.
- 1–3 MPH: Light air. Small ripples on lake. You can tell wind direction only by watching smoke as it drifts off, or by observing light

items like feathers, dust or grass clippings dropped from the hand. This wind will not register on weather vanes.

- 4–7 MPH: Light breeze. Wind can be felt on face. Leaves rustle. Weather vane moves.
- 8–12 MPH: Gentle breeze. Leaves and twigs in constant motion. Small, light flags are extended out from the pole.
- 13–18 MPH: Moderate breeze. Dust and paper blow before wind. Small branches move.
- 19–24 MPH: Fresh breeze. Small waves with whitecaps. Small leafy trees sway.
- 25–31 MPH: Strong breeze. Large branches dance in the wind. Phone wires jump a little, whistle. It is difficult to carry open umbrellas.
- 32–38 MPH: Moderate gale. Trees bend with the wind. It takes a little determination to walk into the wind.
- 39–46 MPH: Fresh gale. Twigs snap off trees. You have to hunch over and fight against a head wind to make progress.
- 47–54 MPH: Strong gale. Shingles blow off roofs.
- 55–63 MPH: Whole gale. Trees topple. Buildings are damaged.
- 64–72 MPH: Storm. Much damage.
- 73 MPH and up: Hurricane.

The stronger the wind is, the shorter the length of time each gust will blow. As a gust of wind speeds up it moves clockwise (veering). As it slows down it moves counterclockwise (backing).

The Colors of the Day

Almost everyone knows this familiar rhyme: "Red sky at night, sailor's delight. Red sky at morning, sailor take warning." The sailor of this rhyme looks to the west—where weather comes from—for a sign of what the following day will be like. The colors of a sunset depend upon the dust and moisture in the atmosphere.

Yellowish skies at dusk are a result of the sunlight passing through dry air and mean that fair weather is coming. Blue or purple skies mean that fair weather will continue. A pink or light-red sky also indicates fair weather. However, a dark red sky means the dust is laden with moisture and rain may follow. Whitish and gray skies mean the sun is shining through moist air and rain will follow.

Looking to the east, at dawn, a gray sky means that the storm has passed and you can expect clearing weather. A red sky at dawn means fair weather has passed and humidity is likely to be rising; rain is coming. The sky you see at dawn to the east has already passed, so use this indication along with sunset colors to determine what the day's weather is likely to be.

The colors of the day can be remembered by this folk rhyme:

> Evening red and morning gray
> Send the traveller on his way
> Evening gray and morning red
> Send the traveller wet to bed.

(While these adages have stood for a long time, they can certainly stand updating. Try making up something that makes more sense to you: "Red sky at dawn, don't water the lawn." And so on.)

Blue Moon

The moon, too, can be read for signs of approaching weather. It is a good report of the weather aloft. Weather usually works its way down from the upper atmosphere—anything from cooler winds on top to the humid warm air of a new front. If the moon is silver or white, expect fair weather. A dark red moon (like a dark red sunset) glows through moist upper air and foretells rain in twelve to fourteen hours.

On a night when the stars and moon can be seen with vivid clarity, the twinkling of the stars is a sign of strong winds aloft. This is also a sign of cooling weather. It means there is no cloud cover to keep the earth's heat from dissipating skyward. Clear nights like this will leave early-morning dew and ground fog—a sign of a fair, dry day to come. In the spring and fall, clear nights should put gardeners on watch for frost. If there is no dew in the morning, but the air is still and hot, watch for a storm.

If the moon begins to appear dull, with its edges less defined, it is a sign of rain. The rain will start within ten hours after the moon loses its visible outline. The dulling is caused by the high advance clouds of a warm front moving in, bringing humid air. (Confirm this with the thermometer; if it gets warmer between 7:00 P.M. and midnight, rain is likely.)

The following are some fair weather signs to look for:

- Summer fog clears before noon.
- Clouds decrease in number.
- Wind blows gently from west or northwest (east of the Rockies).
- Setting sun looks like a ball of fire; sky is clear.
- Moon shines brightly and wind is light.
- Heavy dew or frost at night.

Halos

In changing weather halos will form around the moon or sun. A halo around the moon foretells snow or rain within three days. A halo around the sun means snow or rain within twenty-four hours.

Halos are usually white, but will occasionally show a red inner ring. They are formed by moonlight (or sunshine) passing through ice crystals at a very high altitude. These ice crystals are at the forward edge of a storm center, part of the thin layer of cirrostratus clouds that tell of a coming warm front. Halos appear to grow and move away as humidity increases and the cloud layer drops—a sign that a storm is near.

Thicker clouds, rain clouds, will cause *coronas*— small tinted rings around the moon, sun and even stars. Caused by light shining through water droplets, these rings tend to be red on the outside and blue in the interior. If the corona expands, it is a sign that the moisture is evaporating and the weather will be clear. A shrinking corona is a sign that the water droplets are growing and rain will follow.

Rainbows

Rainbows appear only when there are heavy rain clouds opposite the sun, usually in the morning or late afternoon. The lower the sun is in the sky, the higher the rainbow will be.

A morning rainbow will appear in the west, and it forecasts rain. A late afternoon rainbow follows a storm and appears in the east, a promise that the storm has passed. If the rainbow is upwind, expect rain; if it's downwind, the clouds are moving away and fair weather will follow.

Lightning

Years ago, during an early summer storm, I was potting plants with my father in our greenhouse. The dark woods around us were lit up by bolts of lightning as the rain poured. There was a flash and a clap of thunder; the greenhouse shook. I looked up. The metal frame of the greenhouse was alive with sparks. When I saw the crackling sparks, I ran toward the door. But when I was a few steps from it, a huge white-blue spark arced between the metal hook on the doorjamb and the metal latch on the open door.

I spun around and headed for the other exit, running as fast as I could. I was flung up in the air as my father grabbed my pants and shirt. Right in front of me was the metal wheel that opened the vents at the top of the greenhouse. "Touch that," my father said, "and from now on, they'll call you Curly."

An average of one hundred people a year are killed by lightning, more than are killed in tornadoes and hurricanes. Researchers are now finding that lightning strikes more frequently than previously thought. Using new ground-based lightning detection equipment, they have found that a square mile of ground will be struck an average of ten times a year. In some areas, like Florida, it may be as high as forty times a year.

By observing distant lightning, you can judge the approach of a storm. Count the number of seconds that elapse between the time you see a flash of lightning and when you hear the thunder. (You don't need a watch. Count by one hundreds: one-one hundred, two-one hundred, etc.) Divide the number of seconds you counted by five (sound travels at about 5 miles per second). This will tell you how far away the storm is. For example, if twenty seconds elapse between the lightning and the thunder, then (dividing by five) the storm is 4 miles away. Thunder can be heard as far away as 20 miles, but it is more commonly heard at half that distance or less.

If the lightning is flashing to the northwest, west or southwest, the storm will be moving toward you at about 30 miles an hour. So from observing the lightning, we know that this particular storm is 4 miles away, and since it's moving at 30 miles an hour, it should hit in eight minutes or so. Lightning in the north, east or south is from a storm that will likely miss you.

One kind of lightning occurs without the sound of thunder. Commonly called *heat lightning*, it appears in sheet form, its light reflected off the clouds. This far-off lightning (18 to 20 miles away) does occur as a bolt, but it is too far away to be seen in that shape.

The color of lightning is an indicator of the weather to follow. White lightning, viewed through the clear air that precedes a storm, is a sign that rain is coming. Red or yellow lightning may mean that you're viewing the storm through drier, dustier air, and the storm may pass to the north or south.

During a storm, never stand next to anything tall. Stay away a distance equal to the object's height. Stay off hill tops and away from trees, especially isolated trees, railroad tracks and metal fences. If you're caught in a bad area, crouch down. If your skin tingles or your hair stands on end, drop to the ground—you are about to be hit by lightning.

Certain species of trees seem to be hit by lightning more than others, but there is some debate about whether this is in fact so. However, folk knowledge and my own experience agree that oaks get hit more than most other trees, and beeches are rarely struck.

Trees that are hit by lightning may splinter and burn, but frequently the lightning leaves a path, sometimes spiraling, several inches wide down the length of the trunk. Many trees survive a hit.

Lightning sometimes leaves its imprint in the ground, fusing the silica in sandy soil into a form of glass called *fulgurite*. Branching out like lightning in the sky, this "petrified lightning," formed of many multityned glass tubes, can be excavated from the sandy soil with care. They are several feet long, usually tan or black.

Lightning has an amazing circus-agility, taking unexpected turns, making surprising (and often tragic) connections. When I was a child I used to go with my father to pick up milk at a number of farms in New York state for the creamery. Early one morning we stopped at one farm after a tremendous thunderstorm had passed through the night before. Lightning had hit an oak out in the farmer's pasture. The bolt traveled down the tree and passed on to some barbed-wire fencing that was stapled to it. Traveling down the wire, it came to the barn and jumped into the barn via a power line, blew out a light in the milk house and then hopped onto a water pipe for its final act. This pipe automatically watered the cows, and the pipe was connected directly to the metal stanchions around the cows' necks. The bolt's track left seven or eight dead cows in these stanchions, quite a distance, some 50 yards, from the oak tree.

Animal Signs

For several years, the Chinese had been expecting an earthquake in Liaoning Province. After a period of frequent ground shocks in February of 1975, animals started acting strangely: dogs howled, cows broke their halters, pigs smashed their pens and bit each other and geese flew into trees. There was another string of ground shocks, and the animal unrest increased. Chinese officials took note and evacuated 1 million residents from the city of Haicheng. A few hours later, an earthquake leveled the city.

This Chinese experience is not an isolated one. There are many historical examples of altered animal behavior before an earthquake: mice and weasels fled the ancient Greek city of Helice five days before it was destroyed; an agitated flock of seabirds appeared over Concepción, Chile, before the earthquake in 1835; and there were reports of howling dogs before the 1906 San Francisco earthquake.

Research has shown that animals are highly sensitive to the many atmospheric changes preceding an earthquake. Homing pigeons can detect subtle alterations in the magnetic field. Sharks are aware of shifts in electrical fields. Snakes have an ability to sniff out the hydrocarbon gases released before an earthquake.

As the Chinese observations show, the signs are there to be read, but in a language that needs a more accurate translation. For now the changes in the behavior of animals and insects before a storm are open to interpretation. There is much disagreement about the accuracy of animal-based forecasts and whether predictions can be made more than a few hours in advance. Following are some short-range forecasting signs. If you observe any of these in your area, you should probably pay close attention to your local weather reports and, if you are outside, head for cover.

With the coming of a storm, wild animals seek food with an almost systematic urgency. Some animals will take great risks. Deer will come out to feed earlier in the day. Rabbits, which are normally quick to run off when they spot you, are markedly easier to approach before a snowstorm or thunderstorm. Cattle and horses will gather up in tight bunches. And if it's going to be a severe storm, the animals will move from the hilltops to the valleys, where they can find shelter. Dogs and most domestic animals will act nervous before a storm. Snakes and other reptiles are more active during the low-pressure periods that precede storms. Fish tend to stay closer to the surface;

however, whether they bite or not depends on who you believe. But most anglers agree that fish stop biting as a major thunderstorm approaches.

Insects

As the barometer falls, humidity increases, and storms approach. Bees go into their hives and mosquitoes, flies and gnats swarm at the level of your face and bite more often. Flies will sometimes swarm on window screens before a storm. In short, flying insects are more active twelve hours before a rain falls, but about two hours before the rain they stop flying.

Spiders, taking advantage of the increased insect activity prior to a storm, will spin larger webs than usual. The web itself is indicative of the weather: the anchor lines are shorter than usual during unsettled weather; when these lines are long, there are usually a few days of good weather ahead. Spiders desert their webs in bad weather, and when they weave a new one it is a sign of improving weather. If a spider is found working on its web during a rain, it's a sign the storm won't last. Spider webs on the grass in the morning, often dew-covered, are usually a sign of a clear, sunny day.

Cricket songs change with the temperature. (You can tell these apart from grasshoppers' songs by their musical pitch. Some crickets produce tunes that can be whistled. Grasshoppers, on the other hand, make a mechanical, scraping sound, with no high or low tones.)

Snowy tree crickets are whitish or pale green insects that chirp all night from low shrubs and bushes. They can be quite accurate indicators of temperature: count the number of chirps an individual cricket makes in fifteen seconds; add thirty-seven to this number and you have the temperature in Fahrenheit.

Katydid calls are somewhat less accurate than crickets as thermometers. Rather than change the number of their calls with temperature fluctuation, they change their call entirely:

- 78°F: full call, "kay-tee-did-it"
- 74°F: "kay-dee-didn't"
- 66°F: "kay-didn't"
- 62°F: "kay-dee"
- 58°F: "kay"
- 55°F or less: silence

Birds

Swifts, swallows and bats fly lower as a storm approaches, feeding on insects they catch while in flight. Insects are carried upward during periods of high atmospheric pressure (clear weather) and are kept low by the moist, downward flow of air typical of low pressure. Here, too, a homily is at hand:

Swallows way up high; there's no rain in the sky
Swallows near the ground; a storm's coming 'round.

Birds on the ground are also a tip-off of coming bad weather. Geese, gulls, crows and robins avoid any flight before a storm, possibly because the descending air of a low-pressure cell makes flight more difficult. Ducks make short restless flights just prior to a storm. Pigeons will return to their home roost unusually early before a rain is due. And loons, unlike other birds, will start calling and then take flight.

Roosting birds tend to face the wind. This makes it easier for them to take off, because it does not ruffle their feathers. Note too, how puffed birds look as the weather gets colder; they fluff out their feathers to trap warm air near their bodies. In cold weather roosting chickadees and sparrows will look as round as tennis balls.

Humans

The human body, as anyone with arthritis can tell you, responds to changes in the weather. The rising humidity and falling pressure associated with a storm front makes arthritic joints ache. The albumin-like fluid swells, increasing the size of joint tissues, making it more painful to move. Low pressure seems to aggravate other pains, like toothaches, asthma, headaches, corns, bone ailments and stomach problems.

The weather also influences our moods, beyond the welcoming sunny days. The lowering air pressure of bad weather reduces the amount of oxygen in the system, making people feel sluggish. The increased humidity brings on irritability and a disposition toward depression.

The increase in humidity also affects hair: straight hair becomes lifeless and curly hair gets curlier. Human hair is such an excellent indicator of humidity that a single strand is sometimes used in a hygrometer, an instrument that measures the humidity in the air.

Plants

Plants are better indicators of climate than of short-term changes in the weather. Often just the names of plants can conjure up an entire climate: cactus, palm and gnarled pine bring to mind, respectively, the desert, the tropics and mountain timber lines. But there are some daily changes that can be noted from plants.

Rhododendron leaves react to temperature changes. Above 50 degrees, they are fully extended. If the temperature falls below 40 degrees, they will droop considerably. Near the freezing point, the edges of the leaves will be curled in. When the temperature falls to the low 20s, the leaves will be rolled tightly and look almost black.

The leaves of the trees in the forest can tell you that a storm is moving in fast. Leaves, in general, are aligned to show their upper surface when the prevailing winds blow; when the undersides show, an ill wind is blowing. (The undersides are a lighter color than the upper surface— usually whitish or silvery, as on the leaves of a silver maple, oak, cottonwood or sycamore.) The whispering of the leaves in the forest is a warning to find shelter before the storm hits.

Plants, dependent as they are on water, can respond to the slightest variation in humidity. Dandelions, chick- weed, clover, tulips, scarlet pimpernel, daisies, hawkweed and morning glories all close up their flower petals as the air gets more humid before a storm. The carnivorous pitcher plant, which swallows insects, opens up just before a storm. Mushrooms prefer high humidity. If you see many of these in the morning, it is because it was damp last evening and you can expect rain. Mosses are highly absorbent. Rub the moss on the ground with your fingers. If it is dry, it is a sign of a clear day. If it is wet, there is high humidity in the air and it may rain.

7

NIGHT

Watchers in the Dark

In years of travel up and down the Mississippi, Mark Twain studied the river intently so he could become a steamboat pilot. One of the lessons he learned was how the night changes things. His tutor, as he set it down in *Life on the Mississippi*, was a steamboat pilot who took pains to keep Twain from feeling as if he knew the river. On one occasion, he said: "My boy, you've got to know the *shape* of the river perfectly. It is all there is to steer by on a very dark night. Everything else is blotted out and gone. But mind you, it hasn't the same shape in the night that it has in the daytime."

Twain, who had "managed to pack [his] head full of islands, towns, bars, 'points' and bends" said it was impossible to follow the Mississippi at night as easily as the darkened hallways of his home. His tutor continued:

> *You see, this has got to be learned; there isn't any getting around it. A clear starlight night throws such heavy shadows that, if you didn't know the shape of a shore perfectly, you would*

137

crawl away from every bunch of timber, because you would take the black shadow of it for a solid cape; and you see you would be getting scared to death every fifteen minutes by the watch. ... Then there's your pitch-dark night; the river is a very different shape on a pitch-dark night from what it is on a starlight night. All shores seem to be straight lines ... only you know better. ... Then there's your gray mist. ... A gray mist would tangle the head of the oldest man that ever lived. Well, then, different kinds of moonlight change the shape of the river in different ways. You see—"

At which point Twain begs him to stop, only to learn that on top of all this, the shoreline itself is always changing, as are the shoals and sandbars in the river itself.

Night: and the rules change. The world is made over. In the opening chapter I said that in the woods and fields (and sunshine) we are all visitors, tourists in another land. This chapter extends the analogy; here, in the world of night, we are on a distant shore. Here we are strangers, dealing with hints of night terror. Deprived of our sight, we rely on other senses. Sounds stand out. The murmur of a nearby creek will seem to fill the night, yet in the day we filtered it out. The night becomes a chorus of peepers/leaf rustles/branch scrapes/beaver splashes on the pond. Reaching out, as we find our way, we are more aware of the sense of touch, and our sense of smell is keener too. Our vision is changed—we use the rods instead of the cones in our eyes—and we notice movement instead of form.

At night more than half of all animals are active. This chapter is about venturing forth from the well-lit places to observe the evening sky and the animals that move about at night. A changed landscape awaits.

Sunset and Sunrise

Night rises; it doesn't fall. The darkness inches up from the ground. Stand on a hilltop or mountain at dusk and you'll see the valleys darken first, and the darkness creeping up the hillside until only a lingering light is left on the mountains. This last light on the mountain peaks is known as alpenglow. John Muir described it in *The Mountains of California*: "Now came the solemn, silent evening. Long, blue, spiky shadows crept out across the snowfields, while a rosy glow, at first scarce discernible, gradually deepened and suffused every mountaintop, flushing the glaciers and harsh crags above them. This was the alpenglow, to me one of the most impressive of all the terrestrial manifestations of God."

It doesn't take an alpine range to bring home the idea that night rises. I used to walk in a large grove of red pine that was planted in the soldierly rows once favored by the Civilian Conservation Corps. At certain times of the year, I would watch the reddish light of the setting sun traveling up the western side of their trunks, making glowing pillars of them. And as the sun set lower, a shadow would crawl up the trunks, the red area smaller and smaller, making them look like tall, flickering candles. And then it would be gone. Night had risen.

You can also see the darkness rising if you look to the east right after sunset. There will be a broad dark band on the horizon. This is the earth's shadow, and it will climb higher as the sun slips below the western horizon. Dusk and dawn are the only times that the horizon is darker than the sky directly above.

By using an old sailor's trick you can estimate the time remaining until sunset. Hold your arm straight out in front of you, tuck your thumb in and turn your hand sideways with fingers together and your palm facing you.

The distance covered by your four outstretched fingers should equal approximately one hour of time left before sunset. Therefore, by counting the number of four-finger widths between where the sun is and the horizon, you will know the hours remaining until sunset.

To check the accuracy of your measurements, hold your arm straight out in front of you and count the number of hands it takes to reach the zenith, the highest point in the sky. Divide this number into ninety, multiply by four and you have the number of minutes each hand represents. If you have six of these hands, then each hand equals one hour (hence, approximately six hours between noon and sunset).

Estimating sunrise is more straightforward. The time between when the sky brightens and the sun rises is usually an hour. And long before the dawn's light, birds—set to some internal rhythm—begin to sing. Even on overcast days, this is an excellent indicator of a new day.

Night Vision

At night the eye works differently. The retina is covered by two different types of light-sensitive nerve cells that are named for their shapes: rods, which allow us to see in dim light, and cones, used in bright light. The center of the retina contains cone cells, the periphery has rod cells. This is why if you stare directly at an object like a faint star in dim light, you will not see it as well as you would looking off a little to one side. (You may not even see it at all.)

Rods, however, don't allow us to see color, so we see the dimly lit world in black and white. (Try separating your navy-blue socks from the black ones in diffuse early-morning light.)

Adjusting your eyes to the darkness takes a little time—about fifteen minutes until the iris spreads as wide as it can to collect as much light as possible. But at that point, there is still more light than the eye can use. It takes thirty to forty minutes for the retina to become fully adjusted.

It is never pitch-black outside. Looking at the night from a dark room, the outdoors is bright by comparison. (And this applies away from city lights and on moonless summer nights in the country.) To test your ability to see at night, have a friend walk past you at varying distances while you lay flat on the ground. His or her moving silhouette will be visible for a surprising distance against the horizon.

There are a number of strategies for seeing in the dark. Wide-angle vision (discussed in chapter one) will increase your peripheral vision. When looking at an object in the dark, look off to one side to see it more clearly. Again, this has to do with how the eyes see at night. Try to use the horizon, where it is always lighter, to get a better look at something. If you keep low, anything moving between your position and the horizon will be silhouetted. This also works quite well against the night glow of lakes, rivers and other large bodies of water that reflect light.

When focusing on a small object, try to limit your field of vision by cupping a hand around each eye, with your thumbs touching the base of your nose.

If your vision becomes blurry from staring too long at the night landscape, bring back your night vision by slowly closing your eyes, keeping them shut for fifteen to twenty seconds, then slowly reopening them. If there is still some blurriness, give your eyes several quick blinks, and if that doesn't work, try focusing on objects at different distances until your normal night vision returns.

For your night walks, get a powerful flashlight with a red lens (or paint over a clear lens). The red light will not impair your own night vision, and most nocturnal animals won't be frightened off.

Nocturnal animals, since they have a greater need to

see in the dark, have many more rod cells than cone cells. This leaves them essentially color-blind and particularly red-blind, since the light-sensitive chemical responsible for night vision reflects red light. You can use a red flashlight to look for animals, many of which cannot see this light at all. If you've taken measures to mask your sounds and smells, you will be able to observe them undetected.

Night-active animals often have larger eyes than diurnal animals, allowing the eye to gather more light. But not all animals rely on their eyes at night. A house cat let into the night will linger near the house while its eyes adjust to the darkness. A dog, on the other hand, will just dash off into the darkness, trusting its nose and ears (its primary senses).

Many nocturnal animals also have a mirrorlike membrane behind their retina called *tapetum*, which reflects back any light that has escaped the light-sensitive cells. It is this mirror-membrane we see when bright lights shine into an animal's eyes at night. Remember that animals are blinded by bright lights and headlights, since their eyes are adjusted to making the most of the darkness.

Animals have different-colored "eyeshine," which can be used for identification. The colors are hard to describe and depend somewhat on the angle of the animal's head, but here are examples of some common species when they are looking directly at your flashlight or headlights:

- Bright yellow: raccoon
- White (several feet above the ground): deer
- Bright white: dog, fox
- Yellowish-white: bobcat
- Dull orange: opossum
- Amber: skunk
- Red: woodcock
- Red/red-orange: night heron
- Tiny white specks: wolf spiders

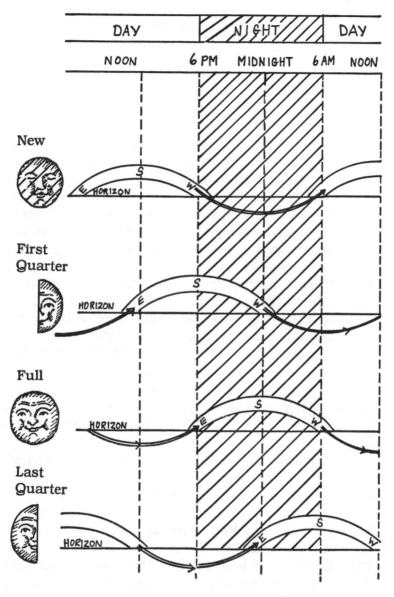

Moonrise and phases

The Moon

The moon moves to a set dance in the sky; from month to month, the phases and location of the moon can help you navigate at night.

The moon rises in the east and sets in the west, like the sun and stars. The time the moon rises depends on what phase it's in. The new moon is not visible, day or night. The first-quarter moon rises at noon and sets around midnight. The full moon rises at sunset and sets at sunrise. And the third-quarter moon rises at midnight and sets at noon. These phases are each about one week apart. As one phase moves toward the next—the moon growing toward full, for example—the rising and setting times get later each night. By knowing the phases of the moon, you can tell how much light you will have at different times during the night. The new moon is best for meteor watching, while the full moon is good for watching migrating birds.

You can also tell direction at night by the moon's progress across the sky, because the moon is due south when it is highest in the sky, crossing the meridian. For the first-quarter moon, this happens about sunset; for the full moon, it's midnight; for the third-quarter moon, around sunrise.

The moon's altitude varies with the seasons. It's high in the sky during winter and low in summer. This is the opposite of the sun's altitude during these seasons.

The lunar phases result from the fact that the sun illuminates only one-half of the moon at any time. In fact, you could think of the moon and sun as being on a seesaw. When the full moon is at its highest point in the south, the sun is due north below the horizon. If there is a partial moon, draw a horizontal line bisecting the moon and extend this imaginary line through the rounded edge. This line points directly toward the sun.

The difference between a moonless night and one with a full moon is striking. Full moons used to be commonly known landmarks of a yearly cycle. The harvest moon and the hunter's moon are two examples.

The harvest moon is the first full moon to follow the autumnal equinox. This moon moves slowly up into the sky, almost seeming to linger on the horizon, moving somewhat sideways. The next full moon is called the hunter's moon. During these two moons, the moon rises almost as soon as the sun sets, giving farmers more time to harvest and hunters more time to hunt. (At other times of the year, the moon's ascent is much greater. In the spring it seems to leap up into the sky.)

The moon often appears to be larger than usual when seen near the horizon. That doesn't mean it's closer to us—actually it is around 4,000 miles farther away than when it is directly overhead (since we are looking across the earth's radius). The sun also appears larger at sunrise and sunset. Why do these celestial objects look bigger near the horizon? This question was pondered by Ptolemy in A.D. 150. Ptolemy said the moon (and sun) appeared larger at the horizon because of an optical illusion: when the moon is low to the horizon we see it in comparison to trees, mountains, buildings. With these objects as a frame of reference, the moon seems immense, out of scale. On the other hand, when the moon or sun is high overhead, they appear as bright spots in a huge emptiness. We have no earthly references to make a comparison.

Empirical tests have confirmed Ptolemy's thesis. Discs of the same size were put at equal distances from observers, one disc toward the horizon and the other overhead. People usually thought the disc on the horizon was the larger one.

This can be verified with your own quick test. The next time the moon looms larger on the horizon, block the horizon from your sight with your hands. The moon quickly shrinks. Or you can shrink it down by looking at it upside down, between your legs. (Thoreau often did this while walking about Concord looking at the landscape, and was thought quite odd by his neighbors for doing so.)

When the moon is low in the sky, it seems to trick us in another way: As you move, it appears to follow you. Again, this happens because we are relating the moon to the horizon. Look at two objects (trees, poles, chairs) that are at unequal distances from you. As you move, it will appear that the farthest one is following you, and the nearest one is stationary. This is an example of *parallax*. The moon seems to be following us because our attention is really on the closer landscape.

The Planets

Five planets can be seen with the unaided eye. The brightest of these is Venus, the "morning star." It is the second brightest object in the night sky, after the moon. A bright, silvery light, Venus is never seen more than three hours before sunrise or three hours after sunset. You can keep track of Venus as the night gives way to dawn. As the sky lightens, you may lose it if you look away. Venus can be seen well into daylight and, according to some, throughout the day. It's easiest to follow Venus when it's close to the moon.

Planet charts, published in the magazines *Sky & Telescope* and *Astronomy* and in many newspapers, will give the rising and setting times for these "wandering stars" and indicate where they will be found in the zodiac, the path through the twelve constellations the planets appear to take.

Jupiter is the second brightest planet. Its white light may be seen for five months in the morning sky and for another five months in the evening sky. During the two other months, it rises during the day and is not visible.

The other planets that can be seen with the naked eye, in order of brightness, are Mars, Saturn and Mercury. Mars appears as a red, unblinking light. Saturn is the most distant planet visible. It has an orbit so large that this yellowish planet can be found in one constellation for two and one-half years. Mercury is the hardest planet to see. It is seen only in the morning or evening, never more than two hours after sunset or two hours before sunrise. The best time to see the lead-gray light of Mercury is after spring sunsets or before fall sunrises.

The Stars

The sky most of us see at night in modern times is a counterfeit sky. The deep black of night, washed out into a sort of fuzzy gray, with only the brightest stars showing, is a poor substitute for all the poetry written about "the dome of the heavens." On a clear night, assuming the kind of sky now preserved in planetarium shows, a person with average vision can see 2,000 stars. But, as *The New Yorker* once observed, there are now millions of children who have never seen the Milky Way.

To see the night sky away from the lights and pollution of this world is to feel as if you have drifted right out into space. But the twinkle of the stars is a reminder of the atmosphere above. Stars twinkle because the earth's atmosphere refracts the light, bending it from its true path. They twinkle more near the horizon, because the atmosphere there is thicker. Stars will also twinkle more when the atmospheric pressure and temperature are low, and the air is humid. Sirius, the dog star, has a wonderful twinkle in the winter months when it is low in the sky near the horizon.

Stars always rise at the same point on the horizon (unlike the sun, moon and planets). A star rises about four minutes earlier each day, rising two hours earlier a month, until one year later it will be rising at the same time.

The sun rises due east only two days a year, on the equinoxes (about March 21 and September 23). On those days it also sets due west. During the winter the sun rises and sets to the south of due east and due west. In the summer it rises and sets to the north.

To find your direction at night, lie on your back beneath a tree and watch a star that is high in the sky. Find a branch to use as a reference point. Watch the star move—it is moving west.

The Big Dipper

The Big Dipper is one of the few star patterns that really looks like the thing it is named after. With the exception of Orion, no place else in the sky has so many bright stars in such a close group.

But, happily, everyone (well, almost) can find the Big Dipper, while bears, water carriers, twins, chariots and queens present many problems, requiring the mind to try to comprehend the vastness of the universe while using the imaginations of the ancients.

Once you locate the Big Dipper, you can find the North Star, Polaris. This is a fixed point in the night sky: Polaris is always over the North Pole. The night sky spins on this point. The Vikings traveled the globe using the North Star (they called it the Lode Star) as their guide. The Navajo called it "the star that does not move" and the Chinese called it "the great imperial ruler of heaven."

Polaris is the last star in the handle of the Little Dipper. To find it, locate the two stars that make up the side of the Big Dipper opposite the handle. They point to the North Star. Draw an imaginary line from the bottom star (Merak) through the top star (Dubhe) and continue on;

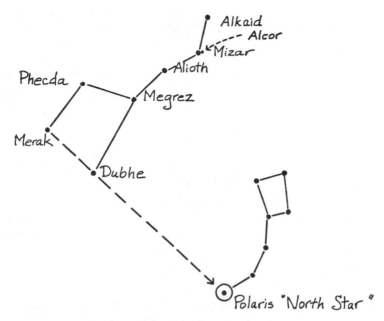

Finding Polaris

the first fairly bright star you see along this line is the North Star. The distance of this imaginary line will be about five times the distance between the two "pointer" stars in the bowl.

The second star in the handle of the Big Dipper is really a double star. The two stars, Alcor and Mizar, are close together, and Mizar is much brighter. These stars were used as vision tests by the Arabs and Native Americans. Most people with normal eyesight can see each star individually. To try this test you should have a dark, clear night with a minimum of what astronomers call light pollution.

Meteors

One of the greatest joys of camping out as a child was to sleep in an open field in August and just lay back watching the Perseid meteors until I dozed off: one, then two, then one ... then wait-wait-one-wait-one-wait-wait-one-one-two. You can see up to sixty-five meteors an hour in a good year. Some leave behind a blue-white trail, still visible in the air the way a flash in the dark seems to linger.

From summer to summer, preparations to watch the shower became more elaborate. First, a group of us set out merely to record the time of each observation. Next, it was on to recording its exact location in the sky. And, the final summer, we made the grand effort to map each meteor on a big chart, which grew damp with dew. With clouds, rain and the general onset of sleep, we weren't exactly pushing back the frontiers of astronomy. But we were heartened by the reports of other backyard observers like ourselves that were printed in *Sky & Telescope*. Astronomy, as is often acknowledged, is one science where amateurs can still contribute.

A few meteors can be seen on almost any clear night, particularly after midnight. But at certain times of the year they are so numerous they seem to be showering from space.

The earth passes through the orbit of debris left behind by comets. This takes place at about the same time each year, and since the particles are traveling parallel to each other they appear to be coming from the same point in the sky. As the particles enter the atmosphere, burning up, they are called *meteors*; if a piece of one hits the earth, it's a *meteorite*.

The shower with the largest number of meteors (about one hundred an hour) is the Quadrantids, occurring on January 3. However, while the winter date makes for clear skies, it does not encourage extended stays outside on a chaise lounge. Some of the better showers are listed below in order of the average number of meteors per hour that may be seen:

- Quadrantids: Occurring January 3, after 10:00 P.M., seen in the constellation Draco. Slow, long trails head east.
- Perseids: Appearing from Perseus on August 11 after midnight. The showers' swift streaks head northeast.
- Geminids: Can be seen all night on December 12, but are best from 1:00 to 4:00 A.M. Fast, short breaks head east out of the constellation Gemini.
- Eta Aquarid: During the early morning of May 4. Swift, easterly streaks shoot from the constellation Aquarius.
- Delta Aquarid: From the same constellation on July 28, early morning. Streaks head east.
- Orionids: On October 20 after midnight. Swift streaks appear from Orion, heading east.

Night Creatures

At night, under the stars we have been describing, more than half of all animals are active. Fish, to take one small example, usually feed just prior to dawn and just after dusk. In the second part of this chapter we'll consider some of the special nighttime activities of insects, amphibians, birds, owls, bats and flying squirrels.

INSECTS

Insects are more active on warm overcast nights than on cool clear nights. If the moon is bright there will not be many insects even if it's warm.

If you want to take a census of the insects in your backyard, use a powerful flashlight with a piece of colored tissue or cellophane over it to attract them. Blue is by far the best color to use; plain white the next best, particularly if the light is focused on a sheet or something that acts as a screen. Don't use red, it seems to be a repulsive color to them. Insects don't favor yellow, either.

FIREFLIES

Each species of firefly has its own pattern of flashing light. Look around on a summer's evening in a field with long grass, or off in the woods, and you will begin to see differences in the duration of flash, time between flashes, color of flashes and how far a firefly travels between flashes. Some species are active just before sunset, others just after. And some fireflies prefer marshes or woods to fields.

Temperature further affects fireflies; as it gets warmer they flash more often, and the flash appears to be brighter. In all species, it's easy to tell the male from the female: only the male flashes in flight. The females are wingless and flash from the ground.

Fireflies (or lightning bugs, as they are also called, depending on where you pass your summers) make an irresistible source for scientific study, and some very accurate observations have been made. One of the most common species, *Photrius pennsylvanicus*, has a greenish-blue, or pale blue light. The males take to treetops and flash three, four or five times at intervals of 2.3 seconds. In another common species, *Photinus marginellus*, the males stay around low shrubs; they start flashing yellow at twilight and stop as darkness falls. The males flash a brighter yellow than the females, which stay close to the ground. A third species, *Photinus pyralis*, make rising yellow streaks of light and then drop down. As the evening progresses they rise a little higher, never topping the trees, making a whole field dance with their lights.

MOTHS

Electricity has been cruel to the moth. Trying to navigate by the stars, it crashes headlong into car head-lights and back-lighted porch screens. Seen this way, the moth appears to be not so much a poor relative of the butterfly as a creature with poetic striving, frequently duped.

Moths use bright stars as navigation markers to keep them flying on a straight course, but they can't tell an electric light from a star. A star, due to its great distance, will remain at a constant angle to a moth in flight; a nearby light won't. In response to the electric light, the moth keeps correcting its course, trying to keep the same angle with this false star. These corrections to get itself on a straight path become instead a series of narrowing spirals that lead the moth to crash into the light bulb.

AMPHIBIANS

The best times to go looking for amphibians are on warm spring nights following rainy days. On such nights in early spring you'll see many (perhaps hundreds of) frogs crossing the road. And you may also witness the migration of salamanders and toads as they make their way to ponds and puddles. They will be breeding from the first warm and wet night until early summer. Sometimes just walking along the road near the edge of the woods on such nights you'll hear a world of sounds, many from animals you may never get to see.

SALAMANDERS

In spring, salamanders travel downhill in the direction of increasing moisture to find the water they need to breed. I have seen many salamanders during the warm spring rains of April evenings: spotted salamanders (6 inches long, black backs and sides with two rows of yellow dots running along the length of its sides) and tiger salamanders (varied in color, but sometimes over 1 foot long). During the rest of the year, you have to hunt salamanders out, looking under stone and log.

FROGS AND TOADS

Frogs and toads stay hidden most of the year. Only during the breeding season of spring and early summer do you get much of a chance to see the less common species.

Go out at sunset and early evening with a flashlight and follow the calls that are new to you. Frogs and toads all breed in water, and the mating calls of the males of these species can lead you to swamps, ponds and other bodies of water (sometimes just little mud puddles). I've often located my position in the woods by knowing where I was in relation to a body of water that was home to a frog chorus. I once found a good swimming hole this way.

Only male frogs and toads have mating calls. They gulp in a quantity of air, close their mouths and nostrils, and pump the air back and forth between their lungs and their throats, passing it over their voice box.

Each species of frog has its own breeding season when it is in full call. From the end of winter to the following autumn, there is a progression of "calling" by the different species.

While there is some variation from one region to another and at different latitudes, the following chart shows, generally, when various frogs and toads are calling. Early dates are for the southern part of their range, and later dates are for farther north.

SPECIES	TIME OF YEAR	TYPE OF CALL
spring peeper	March–June	high "preep-preep"
*wood frog	March–June	hoarse clacking "waaark waaark"
chorus frog	March–mid-May	vibrant chirp, like the sound of a finger being pulled over the teeth of a comb
*pickerel frog	March–May	slow, low croak
northern cricket frog	March–July	cricketlike "kick-kick"
eastern spadefoot toad	March–August	"wank-wank"
*gray tree frog	late April–August	loud, resonant "kreeenk"
*green frog	April–August	"plunk," like loose banjo string
northern leopard frog	April–mid-May	humanlike snore
Fowler's toad	mid-April–mid-August	loud bleating "waaah"
American toad	late April–late July	sweet, long trilling whistle
bullfrog	late June–August	"jug-o-rum"

* call both day and night

Sometimes, even before the snow has completely melted, the first frogs begin to call. In my area, these are the spring peepers, which will call from every water-filled swamp, marsh or ditch. They are most active at night, but they may sing on overcast afternoons.

The spring peepers' call can carry for as much as half a mile. They sing in chorus over and over, stopping only when frightened. Many people think the call is made by insects.

For all this noise, the peepers are surprisingly small. They are no more than an inch or two long with a distinctive X on their backs. They are usually brown, but may also be pale brown, green or even gray.

Peepers seem to call from hiding places while the weather is still cold. As it warms up they are more visible, though it is never easy to get near them. They sing from small, shallow bodies of water, in the shallows or from perches on shrubs or grasses near the water. I've never heard them sing from large ponds, let alone lakes.

These animals are special to me. There was a small marsh about 100 yards from the house where I grew up. And on several nights each spring when the windows were left open, late at night when the whole house was quiet and dark, I would lie in my bed, looking at the moon, smell the breeze from the woods, and from the marsh came the musical chorus of peepers. Whenever I hear them I can picture myself as that child in the dark, under the moon, with the peepers.

At the same time and sometimes before you hear the spring peepers calling, listen for a deeper pitched call ("waaark waaark"). This is the call of the wood frog. Their season is short. They call for only two weeks.

Often wood frogs begin calling as soon as the ice has melted from the ponds. Floating near the surface they call out: a combination of a hoarse clacking and the creaking of a door on rusty hinges. When calling in groups they make rapid quacking sounds like a large number of ducks, cranked up to 78 RPM. The call can be heard for less than 100 yards. It doesn't seem to carry very well.

Chorus frogs usually come out shortly after the peepers. They call day and night, except in the early morning. The sound of chorus frogs is something like the sound of someone rubbing their fingers down the teeth of a comb.

From midspring to midsummer listen for the clicking or chirping call of the cricket frog around the water. The call sounds cricketlike to some, while to others it sounds like two small stones being tapped together. At times you can get a chorus of these frogs calling ("tik-tik") by tapping two stones lightly together. This is most effective at dusk.

Not long after the wood frogs and spring peepers are in full song, the American toad begins to call: a high-pitched trilling note, lasting up to half a minute. This call has a flutelike quality and is repeated for hours on end, making a very eerie, yet somehow melodious song.

Toads prefer shallow water for mating and will lay their eggs in the slightest puddle. In dry years this can doom the long strings of eggs, wrapped around submerged plants. (Frog spawn, in contrast, floats freely.) When the young frogs and toads leave the water, they are miniatures of the adults. All at once the woods will be alive with these little animals.

The last frogs you'll hear singing are the bullfrog and the green frog. The bullfrog calls "jug-o-rum"—a big sound from a big frog. The green frog's call is a twangy "plunk." They sing after the breeding season long into summer. These species have spots where they hide, waiting for prey. Their calls warn their fellow frogs to stay away.

BIRDS

Many birds fly by night and you can see them silhouetted against a full moon. The best viewing is when the moon is near the horizon, lighting up the lower sky. Night-migrating birds travel at an average altitude of 3,000 feet. They usually don't begin the journey until after 10:00 P.M. The number of birds increases and peaks around midnight, when, unfortunately, the full moon has risen quite high. Rails, nuthatches, wrens, orioles and wood-cocks are a few of the birds that migrate only at night. Others you may see or hear—including ducks, geese and loons—migrate both day and night.

In the midst of the migratory bird season, naturalist Edwin Way Teale once spent a night on the Empire State Building. He didn't see too much but heard a great deal: whistlings, honkings, twitterings of birds heading south and occasionally the rustle of a bird settling nearby for rest. Sometimes he saw the birds in outline against the moon, or saw their reflections in the moonlight on the Hudson River.

OWLS

Owls make many more sounds than just "who." Screech owls make a mournful quavering "whe-e-e-eee-oh." Barn owls have a hissing "ssshhhish." Other owls scream, cluck and whistle. And a few like the barred owl and great horned owl, do say "who, who."

Owls are hard to find during the day (unless crows lead you to them). They roost in the high branches of coniferous trees, usually near the trunk. At sunset they fly to perches and survey their hunting area. You can hear an owl call from more than a mile away.

Two owls commonly "hoot" or "who." The great horned owl, which ranges from deep woods to city parks, has a deep voice, perhaps the lowest note you will hear in the forest. The call is usually a deep, "hoo-hoohoo-hoo-hoo-ooo" (usually six notes). The barred owl has a higher pitched call, with a drop in pitch at the very end. Barred owls live deep in deciduous, swampy woodlands and may call on overcast days.

In open country you may hear the "whee-you" call of the long-eared owl. This call is repeated several times rapidly. It roosts mostly in evergreens and hunts in open ground areas at dusk and dawn.

In January and February, you may hear an odd call consisting of a variety of screams, cackles and hoots. This noise is probably the love song of the male and female great horned owl, perched close together. It may also be their young screaming for food.

OTHER NIGHT CALLS

The mating call of the American bittern may be heard during spring evenings. It sounds like someone is working an old hand pump: "cloong-ka-choonk." The bittern's habitat is usually in marshes or near ponds. At least half its call ("choonk") will carry for over a half mile, sounding like someone is using a sledgehammer to drive wooden stakes into soft ground.

Nighthawks take to the air before dusk in pursuit of insects. In flight they call "peent." They can be seen in cities as well as open wild areas. Heated city air carries insects aloft, and these ground-nesting birds find gravel-covered roofs just the place to lay eggs.

Chimney swifts are also town dwellers. After sundown, look for large flocks of chimney swifts over buildings, especially in spring or late summer. These birds roost communally in chimneys, and at dusk there will be hundreds, all chattering, spinning as if in a whirlpool as they enter a chimney.

The black-crowned night heron has a harsh guttural "quark." The yellow-crowned night heron has a little higher pitch, a bit more like "quak." Each of these birds call back and forth to others in their flock as they make their daily trips to feeding grounds at dusk. The yellow-crowned night heron tends to be a more southern bird, and the black-crowned is more common in the mid-Atlantic states and farther north.

BATS

One evening while I was fishing at my local pond, I was watching the pipistrelles, small bats, swooping down and just touching the still water of the pond to drink. This delicate in-flight sip made only the daintiest ripple on the surface of the smooth pond. I sat transfixed watching; one approached, skimming over the water, coming in for a drink. Suddenly something shot out of the water and gobbled the little bat and splashed back down in the water. It was as if the pond itself had opened up and taken the animal whole. A large bass had leapt up and swallowed the bat.

The pipistrelle is the smallest bat in the United States and one of the first bats to take wing at dusk. The following chart shows the procession of bat species throughout the evening.

SPECIES	TIME	PREFERRED FORAGING AREA
little brown bat	just before dusk	wooded areas near water
eastern pipistrelle	early evening	over water and woodlands
silver-haired bat	early evening	woodland streams and ponds
big brown bat	late evening	forests and cities
red bat	late evening	woodlands, street lights
hoary bats	late evening	wooded areas

Bats in flight are hard to identify, but this flight schedule helps narrow down the possibilities. For example, you can tell if you are seeing the little brown bat or hoary bat by noticing whether it's still light out. The little brown bat is out during the early evening. The hoary bat comes out when it is quite dark.

The little brown bat is the most commonly seen bat in North America. Emerging at dusk, it prefers to hunt insects near or over the water using its echo-location system. To see just how sharp this system is, toss a small stone up near some bats. The bats quickly turn toward the rock and follow it as it falls, making those sharp midair changes that make bats a bit unnerving to watch.

If there is no water, the little brown bat will be found among trees in open areas and along tree-lined streets. Like other bats, they frequently defecate as they approach the entrance to their roosting place. The soft droppings are a clue to the presence of a roost, as are the dark brown stains they leave as they slide their bodies over louvered or grated openings. Listen also for high-pitched squeaking— colonies of bats will start this chatter an hour or two before they take wing.

The pipistrelle can be identified by its highly erratic flight. These very small bats (wing span 8–9 inches) are commonly seen in the eastern states. They forage around treetops along water courses, but are never found in deep forests, or in large treeless areas. They also rarely roost in buildings.

The big brown bat is the one most likely to fly into your house. But no need for alarm—big is only a relative term; it is only slightly larger than the pipistrelle. They emerge at late dusk and fly a straight, steady pattern about 25 feet above ground, hunting insects in open areas, among trees in pastures and above city streets. Often two bats in flight chatter back and forth.

The silver-haired bat is one of the slowest flying bats,

with the almost leisurely flap of a large bird. Coming out early in the evening, it is common to woodland ponds and streams.

The red bat is most common in the Midwest and east central states. They are out in late evening, flying fairly straight, feeding on insects between the ground and tree-tops, often near street lights.

The hoary bat gets its name from its many white body hairs. A few hoary bats will look frosted. This is a large bat—wing span over 1 foot—and has a fast, direct flight. It will occasionally chatter in flight.

FLYING SQUIRRELS

At dusk you can catch a glimpse of flying squirrels, their white undersides floating from tree to tree. Flying squirrels are nocturnal and are rarely on the ground. They are frequently nearby, though they go unsuspected. On summer evenings listen for twittering high-pitched voices.

Flying squirrels have loose folds of skin running from their wrists to their ankles. When they stretch these limbs out, this skin stretches, allowing them to glide 30 to 40 feet or more from one tree perch to another, or to the ground. They steer by using their wide, flat tails as rudders.

They land by raising up the front of their bodies just before impact, touching down hind feet first (much the way airplanes land). This upward turning also reduces speed just before landing. The squirrel is rarely on the ground and awkward when there. But in trees it is extremely agile.

The tracks start abruptly where it has landed. In snow there will be large scuff marks where it hit the ground. Its track size is: front feet: 1/2 inch x 1/2 inch; hind feet: 1 3/4 inches x 3/4 inch. It has a bounding gait. And its characteristic trail width is 3 3/4 inches.

The flying squirrel will stay to a home range of a quarter of an acre to 3 acres, foraging for nuts, acorns, seeds, berries and fruits. They are also carnivorous, eating insects, eggs, fledging birds and—if they can catch them—adult birds.

Dead trees are frequently home to a den of flying squirrels. They build their nests in old woodpecker holes and in tree cavities of dead trees with rotten soft wood. The entrance to their nests is usually about 2 inches in diameter. If there are nuts, gnawed at both ends, at the tree's base, it's likely one of their dens. They also build nests of twigs, bark and leaves in tree crotches, and sometimes, in the attics and rafters of old houses.

During the winter, several flying squirrels may share the same nest. They are active throughout the winter, staying in the nest only during cold spells.

Sometimes you can flush flying squirrels from these tree cavities by rapping on a tree, but you can never tell what may be in the hole. Most often nothing. But once I thumped on a large tree with some holes in it and roused a batch of angry hornets.

There are two species of flying squirrels. The southern flying squirrel (*Glaucomys volans*) is found in the eastern states, except for northern New England, northern Wisconsin and southern Florida. It is a little over 5 inches long, not counting its 3 1/2-inch tail, weighs just 1 1/2 to 2 1/2 ounces, and prefers beech, maple, oak hickory and poplar forests. The northern flying squirrel (*Glaucomys sabrinus*) prefers mixed forests of coniferous and hardwoods.

Sounds in the Night

There are many things that go "tseet-tseet" or "yip-yip" in the night that you'll never see. Knowing the sounds of animals at night gives a little more definition to the darkness.

Down by the water, an explosive heavy splat is a

beaver slapping the water with its broad tail, warning other beavers (as well as other animals) of danger, just before it dives below. Muskrats also make a fairly good splash with their tails when alarmed, but this can't always be distinguished from the sound of a big fish leaping from the water and hitting it again.

Something that sounds like someone splashing in a bathtub is likely a raccoon, either hunting, or washing its food.

Back up in the woods, a "tseet-tseet-tseet" coming from the treetops at night is probably a flying squirrel. The yipping and mournful howling you may hear in the East are new sounds. Coyotes have been expanding their range, north and east and into the outskirts of large cities. Prior to the 1950s, coyotes were not seen east of the Mississippi.

More unsettling to many campers than the call of the coyotes are the sudden animal screams in the night. Rabbits when wounded or caught by a predator will let out loud, shrill screeches that can carry quite far. Raccoons and red and gray foxes also scream when seriously alarmed. Bobcats and owls indulge in a truly chilling array of piercing yells, yawls and screams during their mating seasons.

8

BACKYARD BESTIARY

Common Tracks, Signs and Habits

The following could be called an exercise in collective biography. There's a range of characters—some twenty-four animals—about which we know the most rudimentary things: their comings and goings, what they eat and where they live, the size of their feet. All basic information that, when applied out in the woods and fields, can help in assembling a biography of any of the animals discussed here.

All the animals chosen for this bestiary are relatively common throughout the larger part of the United States. And they leave behind distinctive tracks. The tracking chapter discussed the best way to find these signs. This chapter is about the specifics of each track.

Most of these animals share one thing in common: they have benefited from the European settlement of North America. Rabbit and woodchuck, red fox and raccoon, rat and coyote, all are now more widespread than in the pioneers' time. They are highly resilient animals, with an adaptable diet, that have adroitly taken advantage of the newly cleared landscape.

This chapter is arranged by the tracks the animal leaves behind. Hoofed animals, with two-toed front and hind tracks, lead off; they are followed by animals with four toes, front and hind tracks. And so forth. It works from the ground up: seeing a track on the ground, you can page through this section, isolating various characteristics until you locate the correct animal. The track sizes given are average. And the other information—about range, habitat, diet and den—should clue you in on where the tracks may lead.

Hoofed Animals—
Two-toed, Front and Hind Tracks

WHITE-TAILED DEER

TRACK SIZE:
 front: 3 inches long x 2 inches wide
 hind: 2 3/4 inches long x 1 3/4 inches wide

STRIDE:
 There is a tremendous variation in the size of these deer throughout their range.

GAIT:
 Usually a walk or trot; but the deer is renowned for its gallop and leaping grace.

TRAIL WIDTH:
 6–7 inches average

The white-tailed deer can run at 35 to 40 MPH and jump up to 30 feet. When galloping, the hind feed land ahead of the front feet. The hooves of the deer spread apart when running, the half-moons separating at the middle,

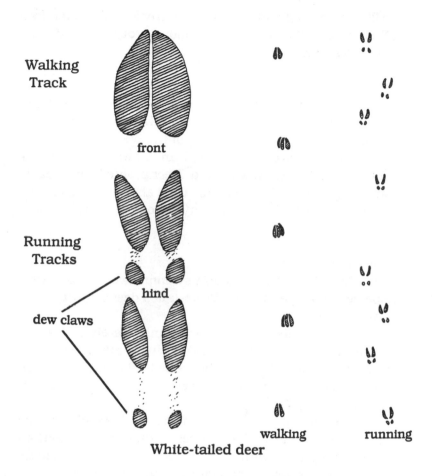

Walking Track

front

Running Tracks

dew claws

hind

walking   running

White-tailed deer

the dew claws making small round prints behind each toe. Dew claws are bony projections raised up on the back of the deer's leg, a little above the hoof. These dew claws will also show on the track when the deer walks through sand or snow over 1 inch deep. They are a little farther away from the toes on the hind feet than on the front feet.

When there is a light snowfall, you can usually tell if the deer you're following is a buck or a doe. Bucks, for some reason, do not pick up their feet as high as does, and they will leave a drag mark behind the track. Does don't drag their feet. This difference is most pronounced during mating season.

RANGE:

White-tailed deer are very adaptable and are found across southern Canada and in all the states, except the southwestern desert and parts of the West Coast.

The range of deer expanded, and its numbers grew, as the primeval forest was cleared. Deer profited enormously when our country's first farms were abandoned and then naturally turned into brushy woodlands—ideal deer habitat.

HABITAT:

The edges of forests and swamps, woodlands interspersed with open fields. White-tailed deer require dense cover.

They are tied to their home range, rarely migrating. Many deer have been trapped and set free miles away, only to return home. They use the same trails consistently on their way to feeding areas, creating well-trodden deer paths.

The size of a deer's home range depends on the amount of food available. A deer's range will be about 40 acres in an area with good dense cover and adequate browsing. In a habitat of poor quality, the home range will be about 300 acres. Deer have a good knowledge of their home range and use different parts of the habitat, depending on the weather. In hot weather they stay in the cool woods or take to the hilltops.

FOOD:

Deer can best be seen in early morning or dusk, and will frequently feed in the same area day after day. They browse on the twigs and bark of woody deciduous trees and shrubs and some conifers. Deer will eat a variety of plants: grasses, herbs, acorns, mushrooms and many others, including corn and other crops.

A herd feeds facing into the wind and grazes moving up into the wind so they can catch the scent of a predator. The white-tailed deer tends to twitch its tail just before lifting its head. If you are stalking them, the tail twitch is a sign for you to freeze.

DEER YARDS:

In winter when the snow is deep (over 16 inches), a herd will "yard up" beneath stands of pine trees, and pack down a central resting area and paths leading to feeding areas. The stands of pines or other confiers, usually found near stream beds, lakes and ponds, shelter the deer from most of the snow and act as a wind break. They return to these yards year after year.

SIGNS:

Limited to their yarding area, the herd begins to eat the less desirable parts of trees. They will strip the trees of bark and eat all the twigs as high up as they can reach, leaving an even line from one tree to the next. A herd can create quite a browse line, 50 to 60 inches high, a sign left behind long after the snows have melted.

Deer have no front teeth on the upper jaw. They eat plants by grabbing them and pulling, leaving ragged edges where they've been browsing. (Quite the opposite of the knifelike precise cuts that rabbits and other rodents leave.)

Bucks, in breeding season, paw up the ground in spots, clearing leaves, tearing up the soil. They then urinate in this area. Does come to these scrapes to leave their scents, and in time the buck returns to see if a doe has been by. These are good places to see bucks.

ANTLERS:

The age of a deer cannot be strictly determined by the size of the deer's antlers. The antlers are a better indication of a deer's diet—how well the range is supporting the population. With good feed, a second-year buck can develop a full rack. But, generally, antler growth follows this pattern: a young buck, one year old, will have small 1-inch-long knobs for antlers and is known as a *button buck*. In its second year the buck develops straight, smooth antlers, about 4 to 5 inches long, and is called a *spike buck*. In its third year it develops a full rack, with the characteristic tynes, called *points*. The number of points will increase until the buck is about five years old and has maybe six tynes on each antler (a twelve-point buck). New antler growth begins in April, and most antlers will be shed after breeding season, usually before January.

Just prior to breeding season, in the fall, the velvetlike material that has covered the buck's antlers begins to split and come off. It rubs its antlers against bushes and saplings to remove the velvet, which is left hanging on the plants in long grayish-green strips. The bark of these plants is quite roughed up by this, showing the bright heartwood underneath.

The buck uses these antlers in fights with other bucks. Antler to antler, each animal tries to push the other back. A fight will last ten to twenty minutes, until one of the bucks breaks off the attack. They then quickly resume sparring until one buck concedes and leaves.

SOUNDS:

Deer make a loud, forceful expulsion of air through the nostrils. It sounds like a combination of an explosive sneeze and a snort. Although deer epitomize grace in motion, their sneeze is truly comic.

CAMOUFLAGE:
     Fawns are born with a reddish coat with white spots. This camouflages the fawn as it lies in the dappled sun of the forest floor. The spots disappear after three or four months. Even the adult buck can easily hide. It doesn't take much of a bush to conceal even the largest buck—which will hide with its antlers low, blending into the brush. White-tailed deer are tan in summer, bluish-gray in winter.

Four Toes, Front and Hind Tracks

DOMESTIC CAT AND DOG

CAT
TRACK SIZE:
     front: 1 1/2 inches long x 1 1/2 inches wide
     hind: 1 3/8 inches long x 1 3/8 inches wide

STRIDE:
     6 inches

GAIT:
     walk or trot

TRAIL WIDTH:
     3 inches

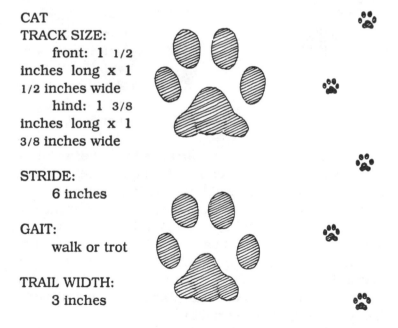

Domestic cat

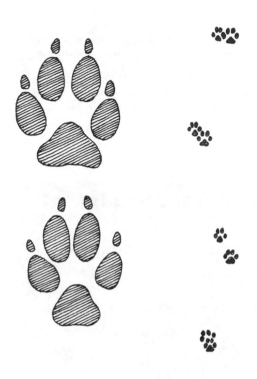

Domestic dog

DOG

TRACK SIZE, STRIDE, TRAIL WIDTH:

varies according to breed

GAIT:

walk or trot

All cats in North America leave tracks that are circular, showing four toe marks. There are no claw marks because cats walk with their claws sheathed. A dog print shows claw marks. The prints of dogs are oblong-shaped. The toe pads are arranged with the two inside toes close-set in the center and the outside toes set back across a small gap. The front tracks of canines are slightly larger than the rear tracks. Cat toe pads are arranged in a neat semicircle around the heel pad, which has a three-lobed pad both front and back. The key to quickly telling the tracks of dogs and cats apart is to look for the claw marks. If claw marks show, the tracks belong to a member of the dog family. This will clearly show on the two middle toes on most tracking surfaces.

Cats leave a straight trail and walk on register, their rear paws gracefully stepping where their forepaws have been. This creates a diagonal pattern of tracks.

Members of the cat family cover their droppings by scratching soil over them with their front claws. These scratch marks are a good sign of cat activity. Dogs sometimes kick up the dirt with their hind legs, but the soil is kicked off to one side of the droppings.

Cats, like most predators, can be lured to your position by sucking the back of your hand to make a squeaking sound.

While it is possible to come across the tracks of lynx, bobcat or even mountain lion, you are far more likely to cross the path of one of the forty-eight million housecats or the untold number of feral housecats in existence today.

The domestic dog is a sloppy walker, dragging its feet, nosing off here and there, marking this tree and that. Dogs frequently travel along country roads, darting now and again off into the woods. At regular intervals they urinate on trees, brush, rocks, mailboxes, car tires. Foxes, coyotes and wolves are more economical with their movements. They cross a road directly, or walk for just a short distance, before crossing back into the woods.

BOBCAT

TRACK SIZE:
> front: 2 inches long x 2 inches wide
> hind: 2 inches long x 1 3/4 inches wide

STRIDE:
> 11–14 inches

GAIT:
> walk or trot

TRAIL WIDTH:
> 4 1/2 – 5 inches

The bobcat's track is about one half an inch larger than that of a large domestic cat, with the same circular

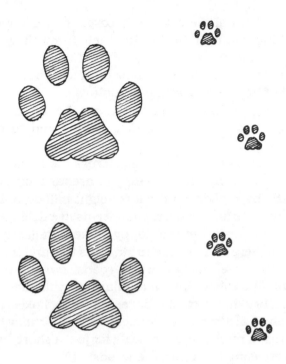

Bobcat

prints, the same on-register walk. The bobcat's foot spreads out as it walks or runs, creating a large print.

RANGE:
Southern Canada, the western states, the uplands of the eastern states and along the Gulf Coast into parts of Florida.

HABITAT:
The bobcat usually stays in an area of 2 to 5 miles. It is at home in many habitats—desert, mountain, forest and swamp, favoring rocky areas with ledges and avoiding largely agricultural lands.

DEN:

Often in rocky areas, rock piles and crevices. It also uses brush piles and hollow logs as dens.

FOOD:

The bobcat is exclusively a carnivore. Cottontails and jack rabbits make up the bulk of its diet. This is supplemented by a range of other vertebrates: mice, squirrels, chipmunks, muskrats, beavers, ruffed grouse, wild turkey and ground-nesting birds and their eggs. Bobcats will also prey on starving or wounded deer slowed by deep winter snow, and on some livestock such as sheep. When bobcats kill sheep, they usually eat the nose, ears and lips first, and cache the rest (as they sometimes do with other larger kills) by kicking snow or leaves over the carcass, partially covering it.

SIGNS:

Bobcats sharpen their claws on trees. Look for scratch marks and shredded bark on the ground. Like the house cat, it covers its scat with soil, though frequently only half-heartedly. If the claw marks are large enough, they may be a bobcat's.

HABITS AND TRAVELS:

The bobcat is rarely seen or heard. It is a solitary, stealthy animal. It is mostly active at night or in those hours near sunset and sunrise. With acute hearing and keen eyesight attuned to notice movement, the bobcat surveys its surroundings from elevated look-out posts on tree stumps and boulders.

When being tracked by dogs, a bobcat will at times climb a tree, run out to the limb and jump to the ground, breaking the scent trail and leaving the dogs far behind— and, as the expression has it, barking up the wrong tree.

Bobcats walk silently on cushioned paws and blend

right in. Their tawny color varies with habitat and season, darker in the forest, grayer during the winter. It has dark spots or bars on the legs or belly and often black lines on the cheeks. It will weigh anywhere from 15 to 40 pounds and be a yard in length. Any glimpse you get is likely to be a quick one, so look for the short—bobbed—tail, black on top, whitish below. You are more likely to hear it: a growl or snarl much like a domestic cat, but altogether larger, amplified, a sound you'll first "hear" in the pit of your stomach.

RED FOX

TRACK SIZE:
    front: 2 1/4 inches long x 2 inches wide

 hind: 2 inches long x 1 3/4 inches wide

STRIDE:
    10–14 inches

GAIT:
    walk or trot, about 5 to 6 MPH

TRAIL WIDTH:
    3–4 feet

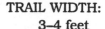

Foxes walk like cats. They hunt like cats, silently stalk-ing, then pouncing. If the tracks show considerable detail, look for a boom·

Red fox

erang-shaped lateral bar on the rear heel pad. Foxes walk in a straight line. In the winter their tracks look as if they have been stitched in the snow; each print, however, is not too distinct, as the winter hair grows quite long on the bottoms of their feet.

RANGE:

The red fox is found throughout North America, including Alaska and the Canadian provinces.

HABITAT:

The red fox prefers a mix of open fields and woodlands. It avoids areas with only one type of habitat. Foxes will stay to an area of less than 3 miles in diameter, but home range varies with the availability of food.

DEN:

The red fox usually dens on slopes with porous soil, in a location hidden by rocks and vegetation. It prefers to use existing burrows, but may dig its own den. The fox keeps a messy front yard: an apron of dirt that has been sprayed out of the hole, along with the bones and feathers and fur of old dinners. The red fox only resides in a den when it is with its young.

FOOD:

Mice and voles are the main food of the red fox, but it also feeds on other small animals, such as rabbits and frogs. In winter, carrion is a staple. Berries, fruits and eggs round out the diet. Foxes hide surplus food near trails, buried under snow and marked with urine.

SIGNS:

The red fox is most vocal during its breeding season, January and February. It growls and barks, but the most frequent sound I've heard is a high-pitched yip.

The red fox, like foxes in general, does quite a bit of digging when hunting mice and voles. They leave rectangular holes about 3 inches deep.

Nocturnal and solitary, it is best seen in the evening or early morning—though I've seen a few in later afternoon in sparsely populated areas.

The red fox, if you are lucky enough to see one, is not always red. There are several color variations. These are most pronounced in the northern part of their range. But most red foxes are red, ranging from a sandy color to a deep red, with white underneath, on chin and neck, chest and underbelly. Their feet and the backs of the ears are black. In the cross phase, the fox will have a dark brown area across its shoulders and down the spine. The fur will be all black in the black phase. And in the silver phase, the black fur will be tipped with silver. There are other color variations, though those are rare.

With such a range of colors, it can be difficult to tell a red fox from a gray fox. However, the red fox, no matter what color, always has a white tip on its tail; and the gray fox always has a black tip.

GRAY FOX

TRACK SIZE:
    front: 1 7/8 inches long x 1 1/2 inches wide
    hind: 1 3/4 inches long x 1 1/2 inches wide

STRIDE:
    6-12 inches

GAIT:
    walk or trot

TRAIL WIDTH:
    3 1/2 inches

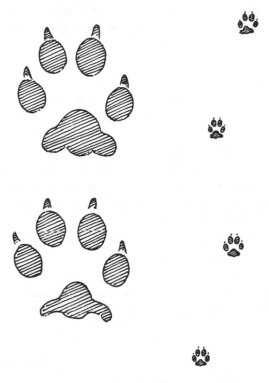

Gray fox

Like the red fox, the gray fox leaves a trail that is a straight line, four toes front and hind, claws showing. The tracks of the gray fox tend to lack detail, particularly in the hind feet.

RANGE:

In colonial America, the gray fox was common and the red fox was believed to be nonexistent. But red foxes were imported from England to be used in the traditional fox hunt. With the clearing of the forests, the red fox became more common while the gray fox population decreased. Today the range of the gray fox is expanding northward, following the spread of the cottontail rabbit. The gray fox is found throughout the United States, except for Idaho, Wyoming and Montana.

HABITAT:

The gray fox seeks out more densely forested land than the red fox. When pursued, the gray fox hides up a tree or under ground, rather than taking flight. This fox sticks to land of dense hardwoods or mixed forests, thickets, swamps. The main requirement is for dense cover, whether it's brush or cactus. During denning season, the gray fox will stay within a mile of its den. In autumn, the fox's range will extend up to 5 miles. The gray fox is quite comfortable in trees and will nap there.

DEN:

Hollow logs, tree cavities, beneath boulders and, less frequently, in ground burrows.

FOOD:

The gray fox is omnivorous, eating small mammals, birds, amphibians, eggs, insects, fruits and carrion.

DESCRIPTION:

This fox is a salt and peppery gray on its head, back, sides and tail. The throat, chest, belly and insides of the legs are white. The tail is tipped in black with a black stripe on top. It is rusty reddish on the sides of the neck, back of the ears, legs and feet.

COYOTE

TRACK SIZE:

front: 2 1/2 inches long x 2 inches wide
hind: 2 1/4 inches long x 1 3/4 inches wide
size varies from region to region

Coyote

STRIDE:
  14 inches

GAIT:
  walk or trot

TRAIL WIDTH:
  4–5 inches

RANGE:
  The coyote's range is expanding. It was not seen east of the Mississippi prior to 1950, but today it can be found throughout the United States and parts of Canada. It is still, however, an uncommon sight along the northeastern seaboard states, in southeastern states and northeast Canada.

HABITAT:
  Coyotes prefer open country for hunting and secluded sites for dens. They can be found in woodlands, deserts, mountains, prairies, farm country and even the outskirts of cities. The coyote, like the rat and raccoon, seems to profit from human habitation. In cities it raids garbage. The home range is about 5 miles during times of abundant food supply, and can extend up to 40 miles in leaner times.

DEN:

A coyote will excavate a burrow in a well-hidden site on a bushy slope or rock ledge. Sometimes the coyote will use the hollow logs or the burrow of another animal, such as the badger.

FOOD:

The coyote will eat almost anything that comes its way, animal or vegetable. It is an opportunistic omnivore. Its primary diet consists of small mammals, birds, fruits, invertebrates and carrion. In winter it eats mostly rabbits. Coyotes can kill deer, as well as poultry and livestock. It will cache uneaten food.

HABITS AND TRAVELS:

The coyote is known for its howl: an opening of a few staccato barks or high-pitched yaps followed by a howl that quavers and varies in pitch. Its high-pitched call is said by some to span two octaves, and is much higher than the wolf's. They howl singly or in groups. If you let out a howl yourself, you can sometimes get a resounding response.

J. Frank Dobie grew up in the brush country of Texas. To him and the Mexican cowboys he worked with the coyote was "the father of song-making" and its song was welcome. He tells of lone Mexican cowboys singing to a coyote in the distance, and of those who claimed they could foretell the end of a drought by the coyote's song. He talks of the affinity that the Zuni, Seri and Navaho had for the animal. Dobie says that though the coyote's singing un-nerved many new settlers pressed close to the campfire, to him it was the "voice of the away-and-away-out beyond. ... If I could I would go to bed every night with coyotes' voices in my ears and with them greet the gray light of dawn."

The coyote is as big as a medium-sized dog, usually gray or reddish gray, with a much bushier tail. It has been timed running more than 30 MPH, with a top recording of

43 MPH. It is most active during the morning, evening and night, though it can be seen during the day.

On first sighting, the coyote can be confused with a timber wolf. But the coyote is smaller, about one half the weight of the wolf, and has longer, more pointed ears. The coyote usually runs with its tail down, while the wolf runs with its tail straight out.

In the past few years in the Northeast, as the coyote spread its range, there have been many stories of "coydogs"—offspring of coyotes and dogs. Coyotes do mate with several large breeds of domesticated dogs (German shepherds, collies, Airedales, for example). But "coydogs" make up only a small percentage of all captured coyotes. This may be due to the higher mortality rate of "coydogs": male dogs, outsiders to coyote society, will not stay around to help the female feed the litter.

COTTONTAIL RABBIT

TRACK SIZE:
> front: 1 inch long x 1 inch wide
> hind: 3 1/2 inches long x 1 inch wide

STRIDE:
> 9–11 inches

GAIT:
> gallop

TRAIL WIDTH:
> 5 inches

The cottontail's two hind tracks are long and oval. Between and slightly behind them will be the two almost circular tracks of the forefoot prints. The left forefoot usually lands about 1 inch behind the right one.

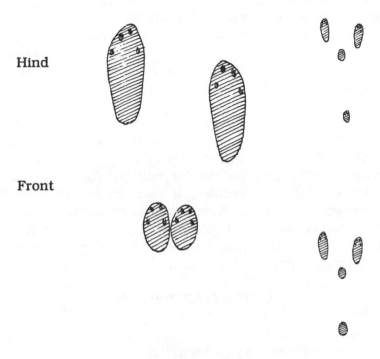

Hind

Front

Cottontail rabbit

The tracks of a rabbit on the run are different. Then, the tracks are in a Y form, the two forefeet forming the stem of the Y, and to the outside and ahead, the hind track prints. When a rabbit runs, its hind feet reach out entirely in front of its forepaws. It pushes off with its strong back legs, lands on its front feet, brings its back feet forward of the front feet and pushes off again.

RANGE:

The cottontail rabbit is the most common of all members of the rabbit family. It is found in all states east of the Rocky Mountains. An abundance of rabbits means there will be an abundance of predators. Early settlers found cottontails scarce. The rabbits extended their range with the advance of pioneer agriculture.

HABITAT:

The adjoining shrubbery of suburban backyards forms a greensward for rabbits. This reflects, in miniature, the rabbits' favored habitats: pastures, open fields, open woodlands, edges of forests and swamps, weed patches.

Cottontails have small home territories, which they seem to know quite well. They are reluctant to leave their home range, and even when pursued will circle back within their area. This makes rabbits good subjects for stalking practice. In a contained area it is hard to keep one in sight, but it will always be someplace close by, watching you. When flushed out it will run in a circle, staying to its territory.

The home range will be as small as an acre or as large as 25 acres. The range size fluctuates with changes in the population. A rabbit out foraging will zig-zag all over the place, leading many people to think their land is infested with rabbits.

DEN:

Cottontails use the vacant burrows of other animals or dig their own nests. They dig a shallow, slanting hole in soft ground, usually in a grassy place that is well concealed by surrounding vegetation. The mother lines the nest with leaves, grass and fur that she pulls from her chest and belly. These nests blend in so well with the surroundings that you can almost step on top of them before you see them. The mother comes to the nest only at night to sit over and nurse the young.

FOOD:

Rabbits feed on the tender parts of grasses and forbs. Most feeding takes place in the two hours after sunrise and again for about an hour following sunset. They feed in the open parts of their habitat at night, and in the bushy parts during the day. The ends of the plants they have been grazing on will look as if they have been clipped off with a sharp knife. During the winter, rabbits eat bark, buds and the tender twigs of trees and bushes. They gnaw at the bark in somewhat vertical lines near the tree's base. Too much gnawing, and they will girdle the tree, killing it. Field mice also feed in the same manner, but leave much smaller gnaw marks.

SIGNS:

Rabbits leave *forms*—matted, nestlike depressions—in the grass. They rest in these forms by day, always alert, ready to bolt if threatened. The grass stalks are usually pushed down in one direction, giving the form a circular shape. Although I've seen them out in the open, they are most often found under an overhanging shrub or low evergreen, and usually placed to give the rabbit a good view of the surrounding countryside.

When a rabbit is caught by a predator, it gives out a high-pitched scream, and then another in quick succession, until it has escaped or is dead. Often this cry will be accompanied by the noise of blue jays and other birds scolding the predator. This screaming call is easy to learn and will bring any predators in the area to your position.

Four Toes Front, Five Toes Rear

WOODCHUCK

TRACK SIZE:
    front: 2 inches long x 1 3/4 inches wide
    hind: 1 1/2 inches long x 1 1/4 inches wide

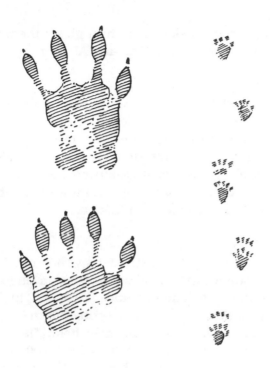

Woodchuck

STRIDE:
    4–7 inches

GAIT:
    primarily a pace

TRAIL WIDTH:
    5 inches

You are not likely to see woodchuck tracks in deep winter snow, since these animals hibernate.

RANGE:

Found from Alaska down through southern Canada, all the way south to Arkansas and Alabama.

HABITAT:

The woodchuck is another species that has greatly increased its range and numbers as the pioneers cut down the forest and opened the land for farming. Before the settlers arrived, it was restricted to beaver meadows and natural clearings. It lives in pastures, meadowlands and brushy hillsides, and will stay within an area about one quarter to one half mile from its den.

DEN:

A woodchuck's den is an extensive burrow. Some that have been studied have been up to 50 feet in length, 12 feet underground. The main entrance is 10 to 12 inches wide and may be placed beneath a protecting tree stump or boulder, but often it is in an open field. They regularly clean out their burrows, depositing fresh soil at the den's mouth—a sign of an active burrow. There is usually a surplus of burrows, and many other animals move in: skunks, opossums, shrews, foxes, raccoons, rabbits. If another animal is using the den, there will not be a pile of fresh soil at the entrance. Woodchucks also dig secret entrances, digging from the inside out, so there is no tell-tale dirt mound near the entrance.

If you get between a woodchuck and its den, it will sometimes charge for its hole, chattering wildly. This happened to me quite often in the cow pasture I used to cross as a boy. I'd be startled by the noise of an animal erupting from the high grass, clicking and chattering, a fat bullet coming straight at me, low, from a place hard to see.

FOOD:

The woodchuck can be a nuisance to farmers and

gardeners. It eats grass and succulent green plants like clover, alfalfa and plantain. Although it is primarily herbivorous, it does eat some insects.

HABITS AND TRAVELS:
Woodchucks are active during the day, especially in the early morning and late afternoon. They are abundant and can be spotted easily. If a woodchuck senses danger, it may give out a sharp piercing whistle before diving into its burrow (hence the once-common name of whistle-pig). It can climb and swim, but rarely does so, choosing instead its determined, jello-wobbling waddle.

EASTERN CHIPMUNK

TRACK SIZE:
front: 1/2 inch long x 1/2 inch wide
hind: 1 1/4 inches long x 3/4 inch wide

STRIDE:
6-inch leaps

GAIT:
gallop

TRAIL WIDTH:
2 1/2 inches

The chipmunk (always in a hurry) moves at a gallop, its hind feet landing ahead of its front feet. The front paws will usually land one in front of the other. The tracks are similar to squirrel tracks, though smaller, and are only seen in snow in the fall and spring. The chipmunk hibernates.

RANGE:
The chipmunk ranges through most of the eastern

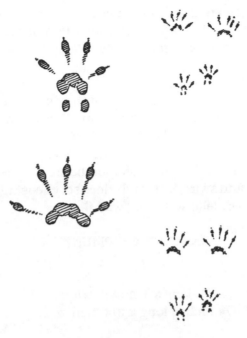

Chipmunk

United States, except the Gulf Coast east of Louisiana and the coastal regions of Georgia and the Carolinas. It can be found in Canada from Manitoba to Newfoundland.

HABITAT:

In New England, it seems every stone wall is alive with chipmunks. The stone walls run through ideal chipmunk habitat: old fields now grown back to woodlands. Chipmunks live on the edges and interiors of deciduous woodlands, brushy areas and in stone walls. It is a diurnal animal, capable of climbing trees, but preferring the ground. The chipmunk will live, forage, mate and die in a home range of under 100 yards.

DEN:

Chipmunks can dig extensive tunnels in soft soil, 30 feet in length or more. The animal scatters the dirt at the entrance, so it is not marked by a pile.

FOOD:

The chipmunk fills its cheeks till bursting (or so it seems) with seeds, nuts and fruits. It also eats bulbs, insects, eggs and mushrooms. It will gnaw through the shells of snails to eat the mollusk inside by making a small hole on one side. The object of all this industry is to store large amounts of food in its den for winter.

Even with its two cheek pockets balloon-full, the chipmunk can sing "chuck-chuck-chuck" without spilling a seed (or "chip-chip-chip," depending on your interpretation). In the fall, and sometimes in spring, they can call with a soft high-pitched birdlike call that can go on for quite a while. A loud chipping is an alarm call.

With a little patience and some sunflower seeds, you can have chipmunks eating out of your hand. First scatter some seeds around and sit for a while. Once the chipmunk gets used to feeding there, start placing the seeds closer to you, reeling it in. Finally, hold the seeds in your hands. This can takes hours or days, depending on how timid the chipmunks are. Once they begin to eat from your hand, you'll be amused at how many seeds they can lodge in their cheek pouches.

THIRTEEN-LINED GROUND SQUIRREL

TRACK SIZE:

front: 1/2 inch long x 1/4 inch wide
hind: 3/4 inch long x 1/2 inch wide

STRIDE:

2–6 inches

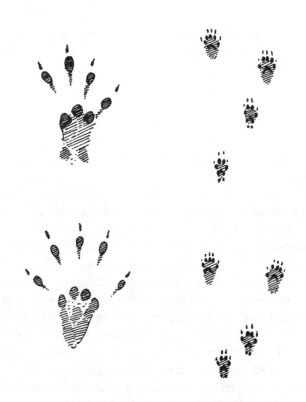

Thirteen-lined ground squirrel

GAIT:
    gallop

TRAIL WIDTH:
    2–3 inches

RANGE:
    The thirteen-lined ground squirrel has a range that
follows the plains, from Alberta down through Texas over
to Missouri and through the Midwest to Ohio. Its range has
followed the spread of farming.

HABITAT:

The ground squirrel is at home on short-grass prairies and grain fields. Its home range is 2 to 3 acres.

DEN:

Ground squirrels make extensive shallow burrows. The den entrance is about 2 inches in diameter, with no mound of fresh soil present.

FOOD:

An omnivore, it eats seeds, plants, insects, small mammals and carrion; also, in season, it eats clover and caterpillars.

HABITS AND TRAVELS:

In hibernation, the ground squirrel's heart rate makes a dramatic change, falling from two hundred beats a minute to four or five a minute. Its body temperature falls too; if it falls below 32 degrees the squirrel will freeze to death.

They are active in the day, and remain in the burrow at night and on overcast days. This squirrel has a variety of birdlike whistles, including its alarm call, a single sharp high-pitched whistle.

The thirteen-lined ground squirrel gets its name from the characteristic whitish stripes on its back. Continuous stripes alternate with the stripes that are broken up into spots.

FOX AND GRAY SQUIRREL

TRACK SIZE:

front: 2 inches long x 1 1/4 inches wide
hind: 2 3/4 inches long x 1 1/4 inches wide

STRIDE:

12 inches

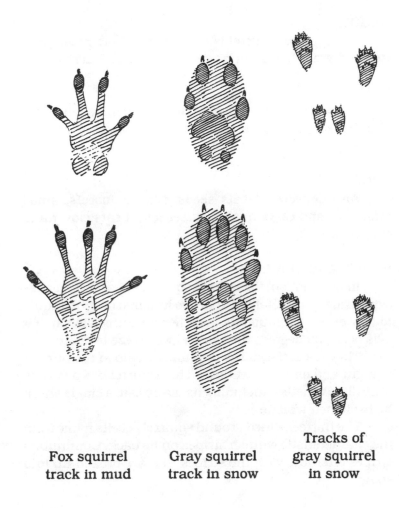

Fox squirrel
track in mud

Gray squirrel
track in snow

Tracks of
gray squirrel
in snow

GAIT:
gallop

TRAIL WIDTH:
4 3/4 inches

As with all tree dwellers, front tracks land parallel to each other. There are usually small claw marks in the track.

RANGE:

The fox squirrel is found from Minnesota down through Texas, and across the South, from West Virginia down into Florida.

The gray squirrel has a slightly larger range: all states east of the Mississippi and overlapping the fox squirrel's range, from Minnesota through eastern Texas and across the southern states.

HABITAT:

Fox squirrels prefer more open land between trees than do gray squirrels. They will be found in transitional woodland areas, while gray squirrels live in more mature, denser forests.

The size of the home range depends on how much competition there is for food. The fox squirrel's range averages 7 to 10 acres. The gray squirrel's, 2 to 6 acres.

NEST:

These squirrels use large tree cavities for nests. Both also build nests of woven leaves in trees, at least 25 feet above ground. Several squirrels may reside in one nest.

FOOD:

Both squirrels depend upon trees that produce nuts for winter food: acorns, beechnuts, hickory nuts. The gray squirrel also favors elm and maple seeds and will also eat fruit, buds, maple sap, fungi, insects and tree bark. The fox squirrel supplements its diet of nuts with berries, tree buds, bark, seeds, insects, larvae, bird eggs and corn.

In the fall, squirrels are busy hiding nuts for winter. They tend to bury each nut individually. They pick up the nut in their mouth, turning it over a few times, run to what they have decided is a good location, sniff around fine-tuning the choice, then, with both paws working rapidly, bury the nut, sometimes pounding it further into the earth with their head. They then carefully cover the hole, both paws reaching out to pull in leaves and dirt and snow; they do this so well that it is difficult to locate the spot, even immediately after the nut has been buried.

Squirrels find these nuts again by smell. They can smell the nuts through as much as 12 inches of snow. Sometimes squirrels will store nuts in big piles in tree cavities.

SIGNS:

While foraging, they stop to eat nuts atop rocks, low branches and tree stumps, where they can keep alert to danger. Piles of nutshells in an area are a sure sign that squirrels are close by.

HABITS AND TRAVELS:

Squirrels are most active in September and early October, gathering stores for winter. They frequently shift location in the fall, in search of better feeding grounds. Dawn and dusk are their most active times.

Both the gray and fox squirrel make a chattering "kuk-kuk" sound while rapidly flicking the tail. The speed of the chatter and of the tail flutter is a report on the amount of danger the animal feels. Danger has passed when the tail comes to rest against its back.

RED SQUIRREL

TRACK SIZE:
   front: 3/4 inch long x 1/2 inch wide
   hind: 1 inch long x 3/4 inch wide

STRIDE:
   6–10 inches slow, up to 30 inches on the run

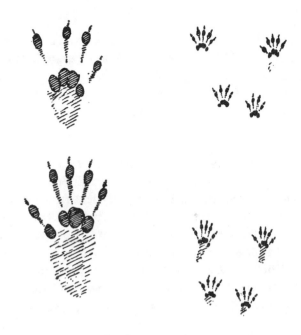

Red squirrel

GAIT:
gallop

TRAIL WIDTH:
3–4 inches

The red squirrel spends most of its time up in trees. The tracks it leaves behind are between the tree it came down and the next tree it climbed up. It keeps to a small area and will crisscross the area between trees with its tracks. It moves with its front feet parallel to each other.

RANGE:
The red squirrel can be found in Alaska, Canada, the U.S. Rockies, throughout the East and Midwest out to Minnesota.

HABITAT:

Lives in coniferous forests and mixed forests of coniferous and deciduous trees. Its home range is an acre or two, or 5 or 6 acres in skimpier habitats. Red and gray squirrels don't live in the same habitat. It is thought that red squirrels drive out gray squirrels.

NEST:

Red squirrels will build several nests in their territories. They use tree hollows and woodpecker holes. Leaf nests are also common. They build these nests 20 to 30 feet up, close to the trunk, in evergreen trees that touch the branches of other trees. The nests are quite large, about 12 inches in diameter, and made of leaves, twigs, bark and grass. They are a little different from the nests of fox and gray squirrels; only red squirrels use grass and shredded bark. Fox and gray squirrels are more apt to use leaves and twigs.

FOOD:

The red squirrel is a hoarder. It stores supplies of pine cones and mushrooms. It leaves the gathered mushrooms in the crotches of trees and shrubs to dry before storing them away. Some of the mushrooms they eat are poisonous to humans (which disproves the adage that you can tell which plants are safe to eat by watching animals). They store pine cones under logs, stones and wood piles—places frequently damp, which keeps the pine cones from opening. They also eat nuts, buds, sap, fruit, insects, young birds, eggs and the young of gray squirrels or any other small vertebrates they can capture.

They have favorite feasting areas where they dine on the cones they have stored. Sometimes they will use the same spot year after year, sitting upon a branch, log or rock, carpeting the floor with several yards of discarded pine cone pieces.

HABITS AND TRAVELS:

Red squirrels do not hibernate, but will stay in their nests during storms and very cold weather. They are most active in the early morning or evening. When there is deep snow, they make extensive burrows under the snow to forage.

Red squirrels may be the most vocal mammals in the woods. They make a number of sounds, but a "tcher-r-r-r" seems to be the most common. They will scold you and any other animal they feel is a threat with loud persistent chattering that can give your position away.

PORCUPINE

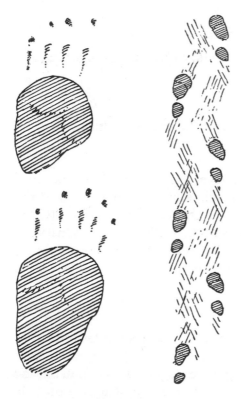

TRACK SIZE:

front: 2 inches long x 1 1/2 inches wide

hind: 2 1/2 inches long x 1 3/4 inches wide

STRIDE:

6–8 inches

GAIT:

pace

TRAIL WIDTH:

8–9 inches

The porcupine walks pigeon-toed, with a heel-to-toe, rolling gait. The foot pads have a pebble

Porcupine

texture that sometimes shows up in the track. Claw marks also show. It drags its feet, which may also show in the snow, and drags its tail, leaving behind a mark that looks as if a broom had been dragged through the area. The result of its lumbering through the snow is a troughlike path. The porcupine repeatedly uses the same trail. Other animals make use of these furrows too.

RANGE:

All of Alaska and Canada, New England, down the Appalachian Mountains to Virginia, throughout the Great Lakes states and much of the western United States except the plains and deserts.

HABITAT:

It stays in forested areas, with a home range of 6 to 14 acres.

DEN:

Rock crevices, hollow logs or tree cavities.

FOOD:

The porcupine is a vegetarian, eating the bark, buds and leaves of trees, grasses, shrubs, numerous wetland plants, corn, hay and other grain crops. In the winter the porcupine's diet is mainly bark; it will spend days in its den and nights in the trees. On summer days, the porcupine stays up in a tree, and during the nights it forages on the ground.

SIGNS:

Where porcupines feed on acorns or other nuts, they clip away branches and twigs, littering the ground below.

Their other calling card is de-barked patches on trees. They may strip large patches off just above a branch. After a stay of several days in one tree, there will be piles of bark, twigs, pine cones and droppings on the ground. Coming upon such a sign, you may be able to find the porcupine still in the tree. The porcupine is black and brown in the East and yellowish in the West. It has poor vision, but good hearing and smell and will occasionally rear up on its hind legs to get a better scent on the wind. If you have the good fortune to see it during the day, it will look like a large, dark, ball-shaped growth in the tree. Naturalist Diana Kappel-Smith, in *Wintering*, described them this way: "Their black faces are strangely ape-like, they have the delicate stiff fingers of an old woman. They peer down at one with a thoughtful, serious look, the sober glance of a judge."

Five Toes, All Feet

OPOSSUM

TRACK SIZE:
  front: 1 1/2 inches long x 1 3/4 inches wide
  hind: 1 3/4 inches long x 1 1/2 inches wide

STRIDE:
  8–12 inches

GAIT:
  pace, similar to the side-to-side shuffle of the raccoon

TRAIL WIDTH:
  5–6 inches

The opossum has an unusual rear track. The thumb, or big toe, seems disjointed, widely separated from the other four toes. The toes show claw marks, except for the odd thumb. The rear track lands by the side of the front

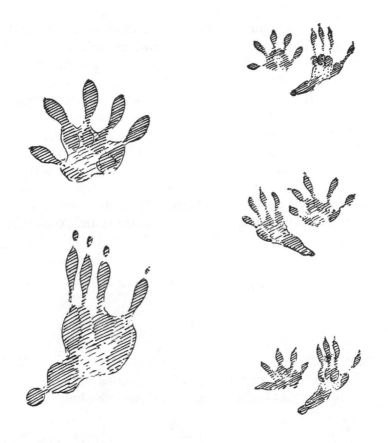

Opossum

track and at times overlaps. In deep snow, the opossum
leaves tail drag marks.

RANGE:
 Opossums are found through much of the United
States and down into Mexico. They are absent from the
Great Plains, northern New England and the extreme
northern border of the lower forty-eight states.

HABITAT:

Given its druthers, the opossum stays to low wooded areas along rivers or swamps. But it is also found in upland areas, and is drawn to the garbage in areas of human settlement. Its home range is 20 to 30 acres. Opossums are not territorial and their ranges may overlap. They are solitary except in breeding season. Opossums are less active in winter, although they do not hibernate. They may lose some parts of their naked ears and tails to frostbite.

DEN:

An opossum will often use a different den each day, choosing from the abandoned burrows of other animals, hollow logs, tree cavities, brush piles and rock crevices.

FOOD:

The staples of the opossum's diet are insects and a variety of wild fruits. However, these animals are omnivorous scavengers, eating everything from nuts to carrion to garbage.

HABITS AND TRAVELS:

The opossum is a slow animal and nocturnal in nature. It pokes around, seems to be out of it and looks dazed and dull-witted. But it's successful. A survivor. It is North America's only marsupial. At birth the young crawl up into the mother's pouch to nurse for several months. After emerging from the pouch, they ride about on their mother's back for several weeks.

To some, the opossum resembles a big rat. Its nose is long, pointed, pinkish. The face is white. The ears are hairless, mostly black, sometimes with white tips. The tail is hairless, rounded and whitish, a giant rat's rail with an exception: it's prehensile. The opossum can use its tail as an extra hand to support itself while moving among trees. Its coat is whitish-gray in the north, darker in the south.

The opossum's slowness conceals its considerable talents—its odd, opposable thumb that helps it climb, its prehensile tail, a sharp sense of smell, excellent night vision, good swimming ability and successful defense tactics. If you come upon one, it may give off a throaty hiss and grin, showing teeth. (It has more teeth than any other animal in the United States, making the skull easy to identify.) If it feels threatened, it will play "possum," going into a trancelike state that can last hours.

WEASEL

TRACK SIZE:
> front: 1 inch long x 1/2 inch wide
> hind: 1 1/4 inches long x 3/4 inch wide
> Short-tailed weasel tracks are about one quarter of an inch smaller, with similar proportions.

STRIDE:
> 11–13 inches

GAIT:
> bounding

TRAIL WIDTH:
> 2 1/2 inches–3 1/2 inches

There are three species of weasels in the United States: the long-tailed weasel (*Musetela frenata*), the short-tailed weasel, or ermine (*Mustela ermina*), and the least weasel (*Mustela nivalis*). The least weasel is rare throughout its range and is not discussed further here.

Weasels leave twin prints in the snow, placing their hind feet exactly where their forefeet have been. At times, one hind foot will be slightly forward of the other. There are claw marks visible in the tracks, and often the fifth toe doesn't show.

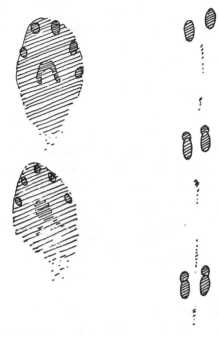

Weasel

A weasel's bound covers a foot on average, and up to several feet in a single bound when moving faster. In snow they often dive below in pursuit of their prey—the trail disappearing down a hole and then suddenly emerging again. In deeper snow they may leave behind tail drag marks.

RANGE:

The long-tailed weasel is found in southern Canada, and most of the United States except for parts of southern California and parts of the southwestern states.

The short-tailed weasel lives in Alaska, Canada, the Great Lakes states, the Northeast and the northwestern states.

HABITAT:

Weasels prefer to be near water and live in open woods, brushy areas, grasslands, wetlands, river bottoms and farmland. Its home range averages 30 to 40 acres.

DEN:

The weasel evicts the tenants of burrows by eating them. Mice are the usual victims. Weasels, even when fully grown, can work themselves into the smallest of spaces— 1 inch in diameter. They also den in natural holes and crevices. When hunting, a weasel will range one quarter to one half mile from its den before circling back. But within that home range they seem to cover three times the distance, zig-zagging while thoroughly exploring all holes, crevices and nooks, hurriedly hurriedly.

FOOD:

Weasels hunt small prey, rodents, rabbits, birds, snails, frogs and insects. They kill by biting their victims at the base of the neck, sometimes severing it, or by piercing the skull with their canine teeth. They often attack the throat of larger prey, bringing down rabbits many times larger than themselves. Their jaws are attached to a powerful muscle that is almost impossible to pry open. The naturalist Ernest Thompson Seton reported this story from the turn of the century:

> *Once a man shot an eagle out of the sky and, upon examining it, found the skull of a weasel locked to its neck. One could imagine the scene: the weasel attacking, going for the throat, the eagle pulling away, all wings, all eagle strength, finally winning. Or maybe it wasn't a fight to the death, but rather a battle of wills, the weasel holding on until starvation, the eagle enduring.*

Weasels hunt mostly on the ground and in burrows, frequently killing more than they can eat at one time. They also can climb trees and swim, though they are rarely seen in the water. Once I saw a long-tailed weasel chase a young squirrel up a tree. They ran up the tree at an incredible speed. The weasel's movements were so fast they seemed to be blurred. The squirrel escaped only by throwing itself into a huge leap to another tree. The weasel didn't follow.

SIGNS:

Weasels pile dead mice and voles under stumps, in wood piles and in burrows, wherever they think the cache will be safe.

HABITS AND TRAVELS:

In summer both species of weasel are brown on the head, sides and back, with white underparts. Both have black-tipped tails. In winter, in the northern part of their range, they turn almost entirely white, except for the black tail tip. The black-tipped tail may be a diversion. Birds of prey attack the black tip, missing the weasel.

MINK

TRACK SIZE:

front: 1 inch long x 1 1/4 inches wide

hind: 1 1/4 inches long x 1 1/2 inches wide

STRIDE:

10–20 inches

GAIT:

bounding

TRAIL WIDTH:

2 1/2–3 1/2 inches

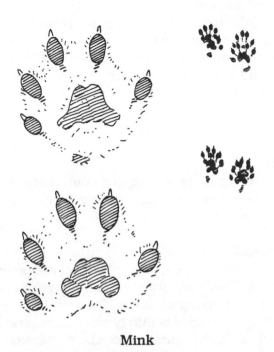

Mink

Although the mink has five toes on all of its feet, often only four toes show, each with a claw mark. The mink is a bounder like other members of the weasel family, leaving paired double prints. It occasionally dives under the snow to hunt or, on hillsides, makes otterlike snowslides. Weighing between 1 1/2 to 3 pounds, it is a big weasel.

RANGE:

The mink is not rare, just rarely seen. It is found throughout most of Canada and Alaska, except for the northernmost areas, and in most of the United States except for the drier parts of the Southwest.

HABITAT:

The mink lives in wetlands—streams, lakes and

marshes—that have a heavy cover of thickets and rocks. Its range is 20 to 30 acres, and it is mostly nocturnal.

A mink will den in the banks of a river or lake it lives near, by digging holes about 4 inches in diameter. It also inhabits hollow logs, tree holes, places under stumps, stone walls and abandoned muskrat dens.

FOOD:
The staples of a mink's diet are fish and small mammals. It also eats insects, salamanders, snakes, birds, clams, crabs, frogs, crayfish and carrion. It often caches food in its den.

SIGNS:
Minks hunt beneath the ice in winter. They are strong swimmers, using all four feet. They forage around in the muddy bottoms, and on emerging leave some of the mud at the edge of the hole or on the snow. The remains of fish near these ice holes is another sign of mink. They do not eat large prey under water.

Minks, like all weasels, also leave a musky-earthy scent. Weasels use these secretions to mark their trail, and sometimes you can smell this long before you see them. The intensity of odor differs with each member of the weasel family, culminating in what might be called an odor gradient to the skunk—once smelled, never forgotten.

HABITS AND TRAVELS:
Once while sitting on the bank of Lake George I was studying a small cedar, a natural bonsai, twisted by the harsh winds of the rocky promontory it grew on. I was very still, studying the tree in detail, when suddenly a mink appeared as if from nowhere, half in, half out of the water. It walked out onto the beach, not a foot away from my hand, and strolled away. The silence with which it broke

the water was uncanny, surprising. The water slid off the
mink and closed behind it without a splash. Seamless.

RIVER OTTER

TRACK SIZE:
>   front: 2 1/2 inches long x 2 3/4 inches wide
>   hind: 2 3/4 inches long x 3 inches wide

STRIDE:
>   15 inches

GAIT:
>   walk or bound

TRAIL WIDTH:
>   6–7 inches

The webbing between toes may not show, but the
claws usually will. The tail often leaves a drag mark. The
otter is weasellike in shape, with rich dark-brown fur and
a furry tail that tapers to the end. Body length is 20 to 35
inches; the tail is an additional 12 to 17 inches. An otter
weighs between 10 and 25 pounds.

RANGE:
>   Otters are found throughout Alaska, Canada and the
lower forty-eight states, but they are not commonly seen.
They are mainly nocturnal animals.

HABITAT:
>   Otters live near bodies of water.

DEN:
>   River otters dig burrows with both underwater and
above-ground entrances into pond and river banks, or den

River otter

in old beaver and muskrat lodges, rock crevices or under a fallen tree.

FOOD:

The river otter eats whatever fish it can catch; usually slow-swimming (suckers, carp) and very abundant fish (sunfish, perch). It also eats crayfish, frogs and other amphibians, mussels, small water fowl and a few birds and mammals.

SIGNS:

Otters often move snakelike through the grass, mud or snow. They push themselves along with their hind feet, leaving a trough in snow about 8 to 12 inches wide and up to 25 feet long. These slides start and end with tracks, and paired tracks are evenly spaced along the furrows.

Coming out of the water, otters will sometimes roll on the ground to dry themselves. These rolling areas, also used after eating, are places where the plants have been flattened down over areas 5 or 6 feet wide.

For entertainment, and nothing else, otters make slides into the water: furrows in snow or mud on the river bank. There the playful animals will use them over and over. They get a running start, fold back their front legs and slide headfirst into the water, diving beneath the surface.

RACCOON

TRACK SIZE:
   front: 3 inches long x 2 3/4 inches wide
   hind: 3 3/4 inches long x 3 inches wide

STRIDE:
   12–15 inches

GAIT:
   pace

TRAIL WIDTH:
   8–10 inches

Raccoon tracks look like miniature bear tracks. The raccoon walks flat-footed. The heel of the back foot is part of the print, as are the claw marks. The raccoon's hind legs are longer than its front legs, giving it a hunched-backed look when walking. Because it walks by moving both feet on one side of its body at the same time, the left hind print appears beside the right forefoot print.

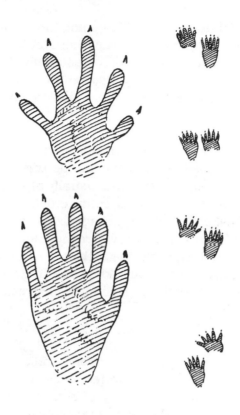

Raccoon

RANGE:

Found throughout southern Canada and the United States, except for deserts.

HABITAT:

Raccoons tend to avoid large open fields and the deep forest. They stay to wooded areas near open fields and water, and wetlands. They are nocturnal and restrict their travels to a home range of under 2 miles.

DEN:

They prefer hollow trees, with an opening anywhere

over 10 feet above ground. The hole can be as small as 6 to 8 inches in diameter. A trail of scratch marks going up toward the hole in the tree or, occasionally, fur around the hole, will tip you off. They also den in hollow logs, abandoned woodchuck burrows and rock crevices.

FOOD:

A raccoon's fingers are thin and dexterous, with a highly developed sense of touch. And this is how we tend to picture them, food in hand, usually dipping it in water. The raccoon is omnivorous, eating crayfish, insects, fruit, nuts, buds, eggs, grass, garbage and carrion. Raccoons are a problem in cornfields, where they climb up stalks and ride them to the ground to get the corn, and in suburban backyards, where they are adept at lifting off garbage can lids. The peak time for feeding is between sunset and midnight.

SIGNS:

Raccoons are good swimmers, and at night you may hear them splashing in water while foraging near the banks. They make a variety of sounds: growls, snarls, barks and whines. They are quite vocal and theirs are some of the most common mammal noises in the woods.

The raccoon is dormant during cold spells, but does not hibernate. It will go out in mild winter weather.

SKUNKS

STRIPED SKUNK
TRACK SIZE:
front: 1 inch long x 1 1/4 inches wide
hind: 1 1/2 inches long x 1 1/2 inches wide

STRIDE:
5–9 inches

Striped skunk

GAIT:
   pace

TRAIL WIDTH:
   7–9 inches

The claws in the front feet are prominent and almost always show in the tracks. The hind claws are less developed and don't show as well. In addition to its usual pace, skunks walk, canter and gallop. When out foraging they usually pace, the hind foot landing where the front foot has been. When they want to move faster, they canter, a three-beat gait that leaves the front and hind tracks on the diagonal. This is a giveaway that you are on a skunk's trail.

SPOTTED SKUNK
TRACK SIZE:
   front: 1 inch long x 1 inch wide
   hind: 1 inch long x 1 1/4 inches wide

STRIDE:
   5–6 inches

GAIT:
   pace

TRAIL WIDTH:
   5–6 inches

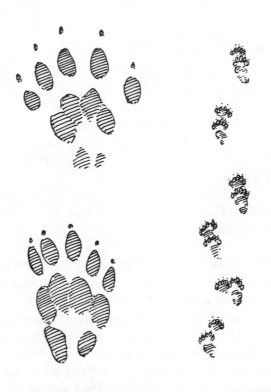

Spotted skunk

The spotted skunk is more agile than the heavier, larger striped skunk. It is also a pacer and a bounder when in a hurry. The spotted skunk weighs only 2 or 3 pounds, while the striped skunk weighs two to four times as much, at 6 to 12 pounds.

The spotted skunk has a series of white stripes and spots on its body. The striped skunk is marked by a white stripe that begins as a broad hood at the shoulders, and divides into a V shape on its back. Both species have bushy tails.

RANGE:

The striped skunk lives in all forty-eight states and in southern Canada. The spotted skunk has a more limited range. It is found in all western and southern states; it is not found in the Northeast, upper Midwest or Canada (except in southern British Columbia).

HABITAT:

The striped skunk inhabits mixed woods, brush, farmland, prairies and often near water. Its home range is 10 acres.

The spotted skunk has a much larger home range, about 4 miles. It will travel about 2 miles a night in that range, in a zig-zagging search for food. Its habitat includes open woods, brush, prairies and rocky areas. It prefers to be near water.

Both skunks are nocturnal. But, while you may see the striped skunk in the early evening or in the morning, the spotted skunk may not come out even on bright, moonlit nights.

DEN:

The striped skunk dens in ground burrows, under tree roots, rock piles, in burrows abandoned by other animals and under buildings. It favors wooded areas near open fields and hillsides that have well-drained soil.

The spotted skunk is a climber, and may den in a tree. (The larger striped skunk rarely climbs.)

Skunks do not hibernate, but will stay in dens during cold spells, two or three weeks not being exceptional. At times skunks live in communal dens, particularly in winter. Frost forming around a den entrance is a good sign that there are several animals down in the burrow at the moment.

FOOD:

Skunks are omnivorous, with insects making up almost half the summer diet. They also eat eggs, mice, grains, berries, garbage and carrion. The spotted skunk will kill and eat more small mammals than the striped skunk. When dining on eggs, a skunk will delicately pierce the side of the shell with its teeth and lick the egg out, leaving the shell more or less intact in the nest.

The skunk in spring is a lean creature. In autumn, after a season of eating, he retires to his burrow about 40 percent heavier.

SIGNS:

A small conical hole in a grassy area of lawn that has no dirt around it is a sign that skunks have been digging for grubs. In a forest of pine and spruce, the holes will look like a whirlpool of needles. A skunk also flips stones about looking for crickets and other insects.

THE BIG STINK:

Skunks run slowly. They have little endurance. They have poor eyesight. They have trouble picking out station-ary objects over 6 yards away. But skunks have that little something that assures them they will not be bothered.

Cross a certain threshold and the skunk will attack. When you get within 10 to 12 feet of a skunk, it will arch its back up and stamp the ground with its forefeet. At 9 to 10 feet, a striped skunk will raise its tail and back up toward you, ready to shoot. The spotted skunk, at the same distance, will do a handstand and, coming back to all fours, will aim its tail-end scent glands at you. At 6 to 8 feet, a skunk feels threatened and shoots its musk—a yellow-ish, oily liquid. They can shoot 11 to 12 feet and have enough musk for six or seven shots. In a few hours their glands will be refilled enough for a small defense and in forty-eight hours the skunk is fully re-armed. If you get sprayed, throw away your clothes and wash yourself off with tomato juice. This works fairly well.

The striped skunk is one of the animals most likely to contract rabies. In areas where skunk rabies is prevalent, a skunk abroad in daylight quite possibly has the disease.

BADGER

TRACK SIZE:
    front: 2 1/4 inches long x 2 inches wide
    hind: 2 inches long x 1 3/4 inches wide

STRIDE:
    8–12 inches

GAIT:
    pace

TRAIL WIDTH:
    9–11 inches

The badger walks on its toes, leaving no heel print. The tracks are very toed-in. The long claws on the front feet usually leave deep imprints.

Badger

RANGE:
Found in all states west of the Mississippi, most of the Midwest and the prairies of Canada, from British Columbia to Ontario.

HABITAT:
Dry, treeless areas, open grassland, prairies, deserts.

DEN:

Badgers are fast diggers. They can just about dig themselves out of sight when in danger and in soft soil can dig down faster than a human being with a shovel. A badger burrow is distinctive. It is a somewhat flattened oval, patterned after the shape of a badger's body. The opening is 6 to 8 inches high, and 10 to 12 inches wide, with a large mound of dirt in front. They favor sandy or loose, light soil for digging. Most badger dens are dug while the animal is in pursuit of its prey. They frequently change dens.

FOOD:

The badger makes its kills in the burrows of other animals. It digs down, in rapid attack, opening the small tunnels of mice or ground squirrels. It also feeds on rabbits, ground-nesting birds and their eggs, worms, snakes and insects. They capture ground squirrels by plugging up all the holes except one, and then digging their way in.

Badgers are tremendously strong and have sharp teeth and long claws. They are short-legged, with flattened, wide backs ideal for fitting through narrow underground passages. The badger is a solitary animal, with yellowish-gray fur and a white stripe from the nose, over the top of the head and down to the middle of the back. It will stand and fight if escape is not possible. And like all members of the weasel family, it has musk glands that give off a strong scent.

MUSKRAT

TRACK SIZE:

front: 1 inch long x 1 inch wide
hind: 2 inches long x 2 inches wide

STRIDE:
  5 inches

GAIT:
  pace when walking; also gallops and bounds when running

TRAIL WIDTH:
  4 inches

All five toes show in mud and snow; on dry ground the inner toe of the front foot will not show. The tail leaves an S-shaped trail between footprints. Small claw marks on both front and hind tracks are usually noticeable.

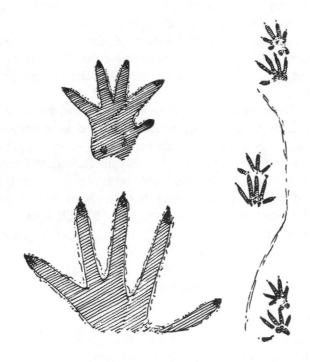

Muskrat

RANGE:

The muskrat ranges over most of North America, except deserts, arctic regions and the coasts of South Carolina and Georgia and the whole state of Florida.

HABITAT:

This semiaquatic mammal can survive in a variety of wetlands: ponds, swamps, lakes, drainage ditches. It prefers stable water levels, and thick stands of cattails and other plants. It stays within 200 yards of its den, usually keeping water near, but may venture farther from the water to feed on land plants.

DEN:

Muskrats construct two types of dens. One is a dome-shaped lodge, about 2 to 3 feet tall, at water's edge or standing in water less than 2 feet deep. This is made of the soft plants that the animal feeds on and is built in the spring or fall. Unlike the beaver's lodge construction, the muskrat does not use mud and sticks. The lodge also serves as a food reserve during times of scarcity. Muskrats also burrow into the banks of ponds and streams. In both cases, the den entrance is always under water.

FOOD:

Aquatic plants, especially cattails, reeds, bullrushes, pond lilies, pickerelweed. It is not entirely vegetarian and eats freshwater clams, frogs, fish, snails and crayfish.

SIGNS:

Muskrats are primarily nocturnal. The best time to see them is early in the morning and during the evening.

The lodge isn't the only muskrat architecture around the pond. They also build feeding platforms, which are rafts constructed from the cut-up bits of plants from the animal's feeding. They sometimes rest on this raft while

feeding. They also leave scraps of plants floating on the
water and piles of mussel shells on the shore.

In winter they construct plunge holes in the ice. They
can stay under water for long periods before they must re-
surface to breathe. Judson Hale, editor of *Yankee* maga-
zine, recalls standing on a frozen pond and looking through
black ice several feet thick to see a muskrat swimming by
underneath him. To keep these plunge holes from freezing
closed, the muskrat pushes plants into the opening.
Sometimes these plugs become large enough that when
the snow covers them they turn into a plant-filled igloo, a
safe haven for a resting muskrat.

BEAVER

TRACK SIZE:

front: 3 inches long x 2 1/2 inches wide

hind: 6 3/4 inches long x 5 1/2 inches wide

STRIDE:

5–8 inches

GAIT:

pace

TRAIL WIDTH:

8–11 inches

The hind feet are webbed, the front are not. Although
the beaver has five toes on both front and rear feet, it rarely
leaves tracks that show all digits. The tracks are often
partially obscured by the drag marks of the beaver's wide
tail. There may also be scuff marks beside a beaver's trail,
from the timber it has been dragging to the water.

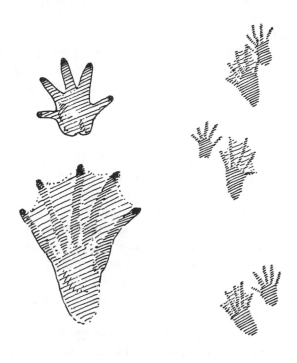

Beaver

RANGE:

The beaver is returning to its historic range throughout North America. Just eighty years ago it was virtually extinct east of the Mississippi. In fact, the beaver had been hunted out of existence in parts of the colonies as early as 1640. But by 1900, the beaver hat was out of fashion, and the fur trade subsided. Today, beavers are found throughout most of the United States and Canada except for the southwestern United States and the coastal ranges of several states on the eastern seaboard. The range has even extended to the Florida panhandle, where in the hot, humid weather, beavers seem out of place.

HABITAT:
Beavers live in slow-flowing rivers, brooks or streams, bordered by woodland and lakes with wooded shores. They usually stay close to water but may travel up to 150 yards over land in search of food.

LODGE:
The beaver is, above all, a fantastic builder, altering the course of streams, slowly damming them up until they flood over, changing meadows into ponds. A beaver lodge is usually 5 to 6 feet above water and 12 or 13 feet in diameter, while the animals' dams are the same height and often several hundred feet long. Above the water line, a lodge is made of piled logs and sticks; and below water, mud and rocks hold the sticks in place.

In winter, you can assume a lodge is occupied if a melt hole is present at the top.

Beavers will not build both a lodge and a dam in all areas. If the water level is high enough so the animal can escape if threatened, it will not build a dam. And some beavers will burrow into the banks of a river or stream, rather than build a lodge.

FOOD:
During the summer, beavers feed on nonwoody vegetation. They eat leaves, buds, twigs, fruit and aquatic plants. During the winter months these animals subsist mainly on the bark of trees. Favorites are aspen, birch, alder, maple and willow.

A beaver's forepaws are quite dexterous. They can fold individual leaves into their mouths.

SIGNS:
Beavers leave many signs of their presence: pencil-point tree stumps, wood chips on the ground and trees girdled with a groove of teeth marks. These teeth marks

range from an eighth of an inch to a quarter inch wide and are usually close to the ground. At times you'll see these marks high up, many times taller than a beaver. These were made, most likely, when the animal was standing on several feet of snow.

Once a tree is felled, the beaver eats the bark off, littering the ground with twigs and barkless trees. Most of the trees they select for cutting will be 8 to 10 inches in diameter.

Sometimes they will build canals to transport these logs. The canals will be about 2 feet deep and 2 feet wide.

They also construct scent mounds along the shore by piling mud 8 to 10 inches high. They scent this ground with secretions from their castor gland, and the pungent odor can be detected quite a way off.

When alarmed, a beaver dives under water, its tail slapping the surface as a warning to other beavers. But in sum, beavers live unhurried lives.

BLACK BEAR

TRACK SIZE:
> front: 4 1/2 inches long x 3 3/4 inches wide
> hind: 7 inches long x 3 1/2 inches wide

STRIDE:
> 16 inches

GAIT:
> pace

TRAIL WIDTH:
> 14 inches

A black bear's tracks are somewhat human-looking, with this difference: the big toe is on the *outside* of the foot.

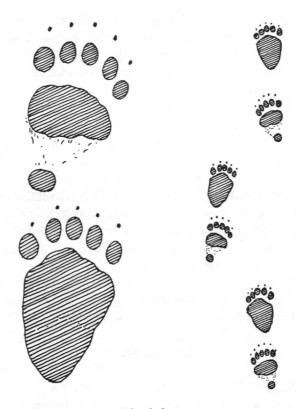

Black bear

Because of its pacing gait, the black bear leaves its hind track just in front of its forefoot track.

RANGE:
    The black bear is the most common and widely distributed member of the bear family. It lives throughout most of Canada, Alaska, the mountains of the western states, northern parts of the Great Lake states, the northeastern states and the Appalachians down into Georgia. It is also established in the swamps of many southern states.

HABITAT:

The black bear seeks out inaccessible terrain with thick brushy cover to escape from human activity and for shade. (Black fur absorbs much sun.) These habitats also have nut-producing trees, like oaks, hickories and beech.

Black bears are travelers and may cover several miles in a single night. One bear, near hibernation time, was 119 miles from home and made the trip back to his den in nine straight nights. Their home range varies considerably, with 12 to 15 miles being the average radius of a bear's territory.

DEN:

Caves, brush piles, under fallen trees and rock ledges, in hollow logs. Black bears tend to prepare a new den each year.

FOOD:

The black bear is an omnivore. The greater part of its diet is nuts, grasses, fruits, berries and other vegetable matter. It also eats insects, especially grubs and ants found under rotten logs, small mammals, frogs, fish, eggs, carrion and garbage.

SIGNS:

Black bears leave their marks on the trees of the forest, ripping off bark, breaking branches, smashing apart rotten wood.

A black bear can climb a tree faster than a man, their claws gouging into the trunks. These claw marks show up especially well in beech trees. Up in the branches of nut-bearing trees, bears build crude platforms. Bears are not dainty harvesters; they reach out, tear off a branch, eat off the nuts, then discard the branch like an old bone into the pile that becomes the platform. These platforms can best be seen in fall, once the trees are bare.

Bears love sweet tree sap, and they tear away the bark

to get at it. Torn bark and tooth marks up to bear height (5 feet) are good signs of bear activity, particularly on evergreens.

They also like fruit trees, chewing off limbs 2 to 4 inches thick to get the fruit, or pulling the branch toward them until it snaps, leaving the tree in disarray.

They turn over and tear apart old logs and stumps looking for beetles and grubs, termites, bees and hornets. Claw and tooth marks are confirming signs. They also dig for roots.

Bears frequent the same trails and will mark a trail by tearing bark off nearby trees. Look for fur under logs (they usually don't climb over). Well-used trails become 3-foot-high tunnels through the brush.

HABITS AND TRAVELS:

They are mainly nocturnal. They are shy around people, avoiding contact. Their inactive periods are spent in beds: shallow, circular depressions in the ground that are well guarded by dense cover.

Bears make a variety of noises, many of which sound human. However, if you see a bear and it pops its jaws together, or makes a sort of swooshing cough, beware: you've got an angry bear on your hands. Don't dally. If pursued, remember: run downhill. It's one of the few things bears find awkward.

Miscellaneous Small Animals

MICE, VOLES AND SHREWS

Up to this point, these creatures have appeared on the menu of almost every animal mentioned. Most animals eat mice. They are near the bottom of the food chain, and there are numerous species of each type. Many of these rodents are hard to identify even if you have them in hand, yet mice, voles and shrews are likely to be the most common mammals on any given acre of the country.

The world of small rodents is a busy one and its populace leaves behind many small signs. Their tracks will show only in snow, mud and dust. Although their tracks are everywhere in winter, like the stitching on a baseball, most of the activity takes places in tunnels under the snow. Melting snow will reveal many of these tunnels, in the lower layers of the snow and in the matted grasses.

Mice and voles have four toes on their front feet and five toes on the hind, like most rodents. Shrews show five toes on all feet. Tracks are about one half an inch or smaller. The trail width of the white-footed mouse and the meadow vole is just over 1 inch. The shrew is smaller, under 1 inch. As for the gaits, the following is a general rule: meadow voles are likely to have a bounding gait, with some walking; white-deer mice tend to gallop and leave a drag mark in the snow from their long tails; and shrews have a variety of gaits.

In any grassy area look for the runways of meadow voles, clear lanes 1 or 2 inches wide, with small piles of cut grass. White-footed mice often put a roof of vegetation on an abandoned bird nest to use as a winter home. Check large brushy plants for these.

SNAKES

I have a friend with an odd pastime. On cool summer evenings he goes cruising for snakes, driving along the back roads of New Jersey's Pine Barrens at 10 to 15 MPH, watching. And there along the roads he finds them, together with frogs, lizards and salamanders—all cold-blooded creatures that have been drawn to the warm road. Blacktop roads bordered by thick vegetation are the best sites. Cool nights produce good results. (On warm nights they may not be drawn out.)

Outside of the Southwest, snake tracks are rare, but they leave other signs. And there are many ways to locate snakes. A sunny day in spring or fall is the best time to go looking for them. Snakes frequently hibernate in groups and wait until it warms up to disperse. In the early spring, knots of snakes may be seen on rocky ledges. Snakes are sluggish when the temperature drops much below 60 degrees. They will not be out on cold days. During very hot weather, they seek shady places or may move near water.

Tread softly when looking for snakes. They are sensitive to the vibrations on the ground. However, they cannot hear, so you can chat as loudly as you want. If you would rather not see snakes, thump your feet down as you walk and they will get out of your way.

POISONOUS SNAKES

When in areas known to be the habitat of poisonous snakes (actually, this is good advice anywhere) lift rocks by the edge farthest away from you. That way, if there is a poisonous snake under the rock, you will at least have the rock itself as a barrier.

Also, if you are walking into the sun when the weather is cool, glance down at the ground on the sunny (far) side of any obstacle you cross. There's always the chance a snake may be sunning itself. In snake country, look well before you place your feet down or go poking around with your hands. Snakes appear to move much faster than they actually do—few, if any, snakes in the United States move faster than 5 MPH—and can be outrun. When several people walk single file along a trail and cross a spot where a snake is hidden, if anyone gets bitten, it is usually the second or third person. You'll know within fifteen minutes if the snake was poisonous. If it was, you'll feel an intense dryness and tightness of the mouth, headache or pain or swelling in the bitten area.

Here are a couple of quick ways to tell if a snake is poisonous: (1) no U.S. snakes that are solid-colored or have stripes running the length of their body are poisonous; and (2) those with triangular head shapes are likely to be poisonous.

SNAKE SKINS

On average, an adult snake sheds its skin three to four times a year. Prior to shedding, the snake becomes inactive and is uninterested in feeding. The snake's colors become duller and the markings less distinct. But a sure sign that a snake is ready to shed is when its eyes cloud over, becoming grayish-white, as the outer layers of the skin thicken. The eye clouding lasts about five days.

Shedding usually begins at the head. The snake rubs its nose and jaws, or makes yawning motions to break the skin away from its mouth. Once it has broken the skin at its mouth, the snake pushes through twigs, branches, rocks—anything that will help pull the skin off. Often skins are found in the forked branches of trees.

Their old skin is always found inside out, like a sock that has been pulled off the foot. The shed skin is colorless and somewhat transparent, but shows the markings quite well. The skin is always longer than the animal that cast it off. In wet habitats, the skin may be stretched as much as 20 percent longer than the snake itself. One bird, the great crested fly catcher, weaves shed snakeskins into its nest.

After shedding, the snake is somewhat blind and is quick to strike. The blindness lasts until the next skin over the eyes becomes transparent. By then the snake's new colors look freshly painted.

APPENDIX

Tracking Test

Match the animal with its tracks below:

1.	coyote	9.	porcupine
2.	weasel	10.	chipmunk
3.	raccoon	11.	badger
4.	beaver	12.	opossum
5.	striped skunk	13.	cottontail rabbit
6.	woodchuck	14.	gray squirrel
7.	black bear	15.	muskrat
8.	river otter	16.	white-tailed deer

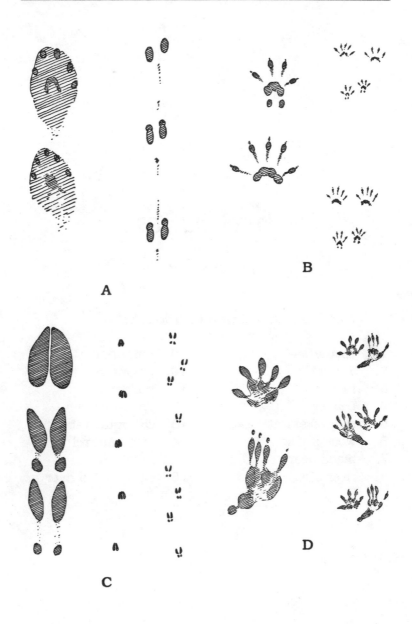

A

B

C

D

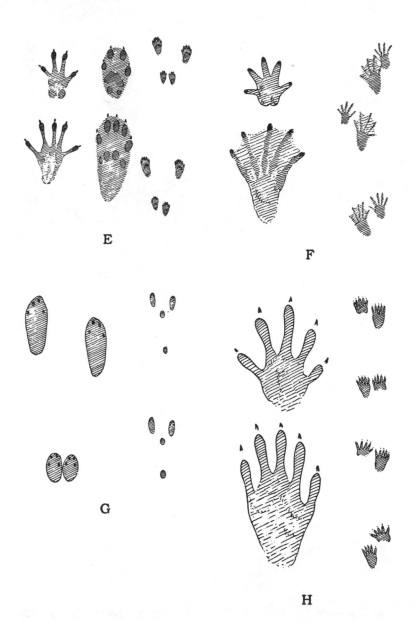

E

F

G

H

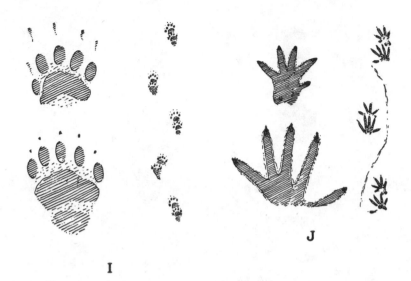

J

I

Answers: A - 2, B - 10, C -16, D -12, E -14, F - 4, G - 13, H - 3, I - 5, J -15

SELECTED BIBLIOGRAPHY

Berger, Andrew J. *Bird Study*. New York: John Wiley, 1961. A good general ornithology reference.

Brown, Tom, with Brandt Morgan. *Tom Brown's Field Guide to Nature Observation and Tracking*. New York: Berkley, 1983. Detailed observations on tracks and tracking.

Brown, Vinson. *The Amateur Naturalist's Handbook*. Englewood Cliffs, NJ: Prentice Hall, 1980. Good for techniques and equipment useful in nature study.

———. *Knowing the Outdoors After Dark*. Harrisburg, PA: Stackpole Books, 1972. The best book on appreciating nature after dark. Includes a comprehensive list of night sounds.

———. *Reading the Woods*. Harrisburg, PA: Stackpole Books, 1969. A primer on reading the signs of the plant community to find out information about climate, soil, succession, animal life.

Chinery, Michael. *Enjoying Nature with Your Family*. New York: Crown Publishers, 1977. Fine source of nature projects; includes many methods and signs used in observing the natural world.

Dennis, John W. *Beyond the Bird Feeder: The Habits and Behavior of Feeding Station Birds When They Are Not at Your Feeder.* New York: Alfred A. Knopf, 1981. Well-written book on behavior of common birds.

Duensing, Edward. *Talking To Fireflies, Shrinking the Moon: A Parent's Guide to Nature Activities.* New York: Plume/Penguin, 1990. A guide to environmentally sound, fun outdoor activities for children.

Elliot, Charles. *The Outdoor Eye: A Sportsman's Guide: How To See, Hear, Interpret the Signs of Wilderness and Wildlife.* New York: Outdoor Life Books, 1977. Many lessons on improving your senses outdoors.

Hanenkrat, Frank T. *Wildlife Watcher's Handbook.* New York: Winchester Press, 1977. Tips on spotting wildlife and the signs they leave behind.

Harrison, Hal H. *A Field Guide to Birds' Nests of 285 Species Found Breeding in the United States East of the Mississippi River.* Boston: Houghton-Mifflin Co., 1975. Photos of nests and eggs, with descriptions of habitat. Sketches of adult birds at bottom of each page.

Hillcourt, William. *The New Fieldbook of Nature Activities and Hobbies.* New York: G. P. Putnam's Sons, 1970. Best general nature crafts book. Lots of thing to do and build.

Kearney, Jack. *Tracking: A Blueprint for Learning How.* El Cajon, CA: Pathways Press, 1980. Emphasizes search and rescue aspect of tracking people, but with a wealth of information on tracking wildlife.

Lawrence, Gale. *Field Guide to the Familiar: Learning to Observe the Natural World.* Englewood Cliffs, NJ: Prentice Hall, 1984. Many short lessons on learning to observe nature near at hand.

Lee, Albert. *Weather Wisdom.* Garden City, NY: Doubleday, 1976. The most complete collection of weather signs with explanations for why they work.

Macfarlan, Allan A. *Exploring the Outdoors with Indian Secrets*. Harrisburg, PA: Stackpole Books, 1971. The secrets here include some good woodlore.

Mitchell, John Hanson. *A Field Guide to Your Own Backyard*. New York: W. W. Norton & Co., 1985. A tour of natural events throughout the year that can be witnessed in your own yard.

Ormund, Clyde. *How to Track and Find Game*. Harrisburg, PA: Stackpole Books, 1975. Written for hunters. A good source on animal behavior and signs other than tracks.

Reader's Digest Association. *The Joy of Nature: How to Observe and Appreciate the Great Outdoors*. Pleasantville, NY: The Reader's Digest Association, Inc., 1977. An absolutely fabulous nature book, sure to interest the reader in nature; well illustrated and full of projects and observations.

Rickett, Harold William. *Wild Flowers of the United States*. New York: McGraw-Hill, 1966. Published under aegis of the New York Botanical Garden. Very complete with great photos and clear descriptions. The twelve volumes in this set provide the best coverage of the plant life in the United States.

Smith, Howard. *A Naturalist's Guide to the Year*. New York: E. P. Dutton, 1985. A look at four habitats (lakes, woodlands, fields and rocky places) through the year.

Smith, Richard P. *Animal Tracks and Signs of North America*. Harrisburg, PA: Stackpole Books, 1982. A thorough study.

Stokes, Donald W. *A Guide to Observing Insect Lives*. Boston: Little, Brown & Co., 1983. Each chapter gives a description of one insect's life cycle, where and when to find the species and the behavior or signs that indicate its presence. Arranged by season. Each seasonal section begins with a chart describing the habitat where each species discussed can be found.

Terres, John K. *The Audubon Society Encyclopedia of North American Birds*. New York: Alfred A. Knopf, 1980. Undoubtedly the single most comprehensive and readable source of information on the habits and habitats of American birds.

INDEX